Praise for The Happy Grades Workbook

"*The Happy Grades Workbook* strikes the delicate balance betwe[en] storytelling. If you think you've seen all the get-better-grades books, this one is different in the most excellent ways! Notably, while *The Happy Grades Workbook* certainly contributes to academic success, it transcends being just another book about achieving better grades.

Tricia possesses an uncanny ability to connect with students on a deeply human level, valuing their overall well-being as much as their academic pursuits. Tricia skillfully establishes an approachable and enjoyable connection with readers, particularly for teenage audiences. The narratives from her life infuse her advice with authenticity and familiarity, rendering it relatable and remarkably personal.

Tricia adeptly distills complex concepts into practical step-by-step strategies that are easy to understand, follow, and apply. While the book's primary audience is teenagers, I adopted several approaches in my own life. Even as an adult reader with a lifetime of working in education, I was genuinely inspired and motivated by the book's insights."

— Morgan Potts, Director of Transition Learning Program, Woodward Academy

"Finally, an easy, step-by-step roadmap for the whole family to create the healthy, happy relationships they want with each other as well as learn how to be productive, confident, and successful in school. Every chapter of both the workbook and companion guide is filled with tips, strategies, and key takeaways, making this duo super actionable.

Tricia's whimsical, conversational writing style makes you feel like you're talking with one of your closest friends who always has the best advice and knows exactly how to support you to be the best version of yourself. The Happy Grades approach is the "glue" that's missing for so many teenagers who want to be successful in school. It not only tells us how to create more happiness, but it also gives us the tools we need to make happiness stick.

The Happy Grades Workbook along with *Happy Grades: Workbook Companion Guide for Parents and Educators* are the perfect combo for every family with teenagers who, together, want to experience more peace, connection, and joy."

— Susannah Cole, Executive Function Coach and Co-Author of *Flexible Mindsets in Schools: Channelling Brain Power for Critical Thinking, Complex Problem-Solving and Creativity*

"I am deeply inspired by *Happy Grades*. It is a clear, resounding call to educators and parents to look inward and find the joy we need to inspire and support our students, or what I like to call the "win-win." Tricia has the rare ability to take lofty concepts grounded in research and make them approachable for parents and educators who want to positively impact the lives of their students and children, but may not know where to start. *Happy Grades* is an enlightening work, that will reshape how you perceive and nurture executive functioning skills."

— Sean G. McCormick, Founder of The Executive Function Coaching Academy

What others are saying about working with Tricia. . .

"One thing I really appreciate about Tricia is how she finds student-friendly language for everything which makes learning accessible and fun."

– Susannah Cole, Executive Function Coach and Co-Author of *Flexible Mindsets in Schools : Channelling Brain Power for Critical Thinking, Complex Problem-Solving and Creativity*

"Tricia Underwood is an exceptional executive functioning specialist who helps students push through mental and academic blocks to find joy *and* success! I have worked with Tricia and been privy to her magic!"

– Rachel Peterson, Education Administrator, DEI Program Consultant, and Learning Experience Program Designer

"Before coaching, I used to be overwhelmed by my schoolwork which led me to not put as much effort as I could into doing homework each night. I frequently napped after school and did my schoolwork last minute. Now I feel much more organized in school. Whether that be my binder situation or scheduling out my work, Tricia made school more manageable for me."

– 11th grade student in Atlanta, Georgia

"There is no doubt that your work with Zoe is having a big impact. She is thriving and, it seems to me, enjoying life more than ever. That's in no small part thanks to you. She's on top of her work like never before and, not unrelated to that, more confident than she's ever been. It's exciting to see her work to her fullest potential."

– Parent of a 12th grade student in Decatur, Georgia

"When he got home from work, he seemed enthusiastic to talk about your session and to brainstorm ideas for how he can stay focused on completing work after school - a time he is typically very tempted to sleep, look at his phone, etc. I'm excited by the progress he will certainly make with you this semester."

– Parent of an 11th grade student at the Paideia School in Atlanta, Georgia

"I feel much better now. When we started, I had a huge problem with not really listening and paying attention and not really having much motivation. And that was on top of procrastinating and having a bunch of work that I wouldn't have the motivation to do. But now that I have a better schedule, I work more regularly and I'm more organized. I'm not getting distracted - well, actually, I still do, but I can pull myself back."

– 9th grade student at Decatur High School

"This is the stuff she's going to take with her the rest of her life. She is so happy. And she's really learning from you. I think she's getting more independent."

– Parent of a 12th grade homeschool student in Decatur, Georgia

THE
HAPPY GRADES
WORKBOOK

How to Improve Focus, Learning, and Productivity Without Sacrificing Joy, Peace of Mind, or Free Time

by Tricia Underwood

Published by How2Conquer
Atlanta, Georgia
www.how2conquer.com

How2Conquer is an imprint of White Deer Publishing, LLC
www.whitedeerpublications.com

First edition, September 2023

Illustrations and cover design by Telia Garner
Edited by Emily M. Owens, Lauren Kelliher

Library of Congress Cataloging-in-Publication Data is on file at the Library of Congress, Washington, DC.

Print ISBN 978-1-945783-22-7

To teachers who hope and try for better for us all.
Your work matters and so does your joy. When you have what you
need for peace, fulfillment, and resilience, our children benefit.
May we see a time when the systems you work miracles in
give you what you need for that.

Contents

Preface

"I hope your life gets even better."

    I found the above note my son's lunch box that was passed along to him by a kid who likes to hand out little, uplifting messages.

    I know you'll find strategies, tips, and inspiration in these pages to make your life even better because everything on these pages has been tested by countless students who have very real issues and challenges just like you. This is my note in your lunch box. Using what you find helpful in this book coupled with just a fraction of the belief I have in your power and strength to create a great life for yourself, your life is truly about to get better.

    Please keep in touch while you work through the workbook. I'm cheering you on from here!

> **You can find book bonuses to help you
> along the way at h2c.ai/hgw
> Find out more information about how to connect
> with me at triciaunderwood.com**

Prologue

Dear High School,

I'm breaking up with you. It's been a long time coming. I knew you way back when and swore that after those first four years, I was never going back. You took up so much of my time and energy and still made me feel like nothing I did was ever enough.

Sure, we had some good times. On paper, you were exactly who I was supposed to be with, and you weren't all bad. My family sure was happy that we were together.

But after years of my life with you, I was done! Done with the worry always hanging over my head about your expectations. Done with being compared to others to judge if I was good enough for your standards. Done with being bored, always having to do what you wanted and hardly ever what I wanted. Done with trying to fit into just a narrow definition of what it meant to be good in your eyes. I suspected there was more to life than what you were offering and couldn't wait to go find it.

The first time I left you, it took me a long time to find myself again: what I liked doing, what I really cared about, the type of person I wanted to be. I had spent so much time doing what you wanted, I didn't even know what I liked anymore. I was so used to being compared to others' successes, that I had to take a lot of time to figure out what being "good" meant to me without your judgment telling me.

I can't believe that after spending the time to figure all that out, I went back to you and then stuck with you again for 20 years! It's just that you had so much potential. I really thought I could fix you. (Spoiler alert: I couldn't.) But I have a lot of hope for you and can see you showing some exciting signs of living up to that potential! I know a lot of really great, smart, talented people who are there with you right now doing miraculous work to save your soul.

Before I sign off for good, I wanted to say a few things to help those who are with you right now. I hope the activities in this book help them have a healthier, happier relationship with you, and maybe you'll change a little too.

No hard feelings. All my best!

Tricia

INTRODUCTION:
WHERE DO HAPPY GRADES COME FROM?

Alright, now that you've opened this book, I'm guessing it was either the "raise your grades" part that hooked you, or maybe it was the happy part. Most of my students and their parents name these as their top two goals: better grades and to "just be happy."

Here's the truth, though: I don't really care about your grades. I think grades are a deeply flawed measurement that does more harm than good. The grading system came from a super old, problematic way of sorting people unfairly for different levels of employment and usually reinforces generations of racist, classist, and ableist systems.

And yet, I know you're living in a reality that includes grades. So while they are still with us, let me help you get yours where you want them to be, so you can feel the relief and confidence that comes from not having to worry about them.

The Happy Grades Approach

The methods I'm sharing in this guide are a little different from the usual study strategies you've probably heard before. But, let me be clear that even though I care more about the happy part than the grades part, following this four-part framework and making it your own will raise your grades.

Now let's talk about the first key word in the title of this book: happy.

Over and over again, I've seen and experienced that when we feel better, we do better. We don't need a bunch of brain scans to know this is true. When I feel down, I don't want to do much of anything at all, and if I try anyway, I make more mistakes because I feel insecure and distracted.

If you are like most people, you will have some moments and days where it's a little harder to feel such positive attitudes as motivated, confident, excited, or connected to others. That's totally normal, and we actually need to have those gloomy feelings for strong mental health. The methods in this book are aimed at helping you recover from those down times with more ease and to be present and kind to yourself when you're not feeling great.

It's totally normal and human to feel down or stressed sometimes. In fact, trying to avoid those feelings altogether usually makes them worse. Like any other health concern, conditions like depression and anxiety disorders need real treatment. The methods in this book can be used in conjunction with those treatments and could complement them well. If you suspect you're feeling down for long periods of time without relief, please tell an adult you trust about what you're experiencing.

Although feelings can come from circumstances or chemical balances that sometimes are out of our direct control, decades of research in psychology and neuroscience show that our actions really can make a difference in how we feel over time. It's like learning to play an instrument. When I imagine a vibration (better known as a vibe), I think of a guitar string being plucked and sending a sound wave through the air and into my ears. It continues until the string is done vibrating. Vibes are like that. We feel them and then they stop, and then we experience another one, unless we just keep plucking the same string. But they aren't just randomly being sent to us through the air. We get to control a lot about which strings get plucked. This book will show you how to get better at tuning your own strings to how you really want to be, and what to do to create a great life for yourself.

How This Workbook Can Help You

If you're getting this book because you have some struggles in school, you're in the best company. You're in the company of people who have gone on to change the world because they had minds and temperaments that are probably similar to yours. People who just didn't fit into the status quo of doing school because they thought deeply and slowly, or they thought quickly and actively. They're creative, uniquely talented, sensitive, amazing caretakers, and idea generators, often full of energy that can't wait for the bell to ring to get out and do something that feels more real.

In fact, it's probably a good sign if you feel uncomfortable having to spend most of your time in a school system that has varied little since it began in early 17th century America.

Right now, we need young brains to be fired up on the right side (the area associated with creative thinking) as much as the left side (the area associated with more traditional school skills like logic, order, and facts), so they can see new inventive solutions to problems we haven't been able to solve with our left-brain dominant approaches.

Left Brain	Right Brain
Logic	Arts
Facts	Rhythm
Math	Intuition
Planning	Imagination
Thinking in Words	Visual Thinking
Linear Thinking	Emotions

And how amazing would it be if these solutions could be created in connection with the right-brain strengths of a sense of peace and joy?

If you are reading this in some happy future and everyone on the planet is breathing cool air in a stable climate with equitable, inclusive systems where we all have a fair shot at opportunity, then what are you doing reading this?!? Go teleport off to the beach!

If that hasn't happened yet, I wrote this for you, so that you can get the education you need from your school while keeping your well-being strong enough to create amazing opportunities for yourself.

Happy Grades is about learning how to do schoolwork without sacrificing your happiness for a later time when you finally grind through all your work or get your grades up. It's a four-part system that supports your happiness *and* your academic strategies at the same time. You don't have to do everything in every section or in any kind of order. But with just a small step that you repeat regularly in each category (that's what BJ Fogg calls a tiny habit, and we'll learn about that soon) you can go from being stuck in procrastination, overwhelm, and lack of motivation, to happily productive, confident, and successful.

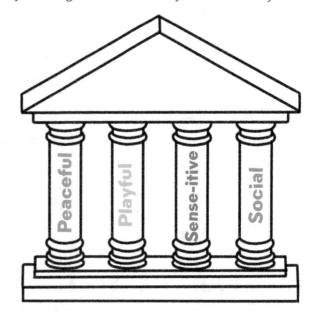

What Are Your Goals?

One last thing before we jump in: for years, when a student would state the goal of getting into a good college as the reason for wanting to work on their habits and strategies with me, a little voice inside of me would ask, "Yeah, but why?" I didn't ask the question out loud because I was scared that the student's resulting conversation at home would get me fired. "Hey, my academic coach said I don't have to go to college to be successful! The world is changing and in fact has already changed, and all this stuff you and my guidance counselor at school tell me to do to stay on track might not actually work after all!"

So, let me be clear about this now, and it's totally okay if you disagree. Yes, following the advice in this book will raise your grades, but you will get so much farther with your success and happiness if your goal for raising your grades goes further than "to get into college." I don't believe that going to a "good" four-year college after high school is the only path to success or security. And what's more, I think you've seen too much proof that there are lots of different paths, that you might have questioned that belief, too.

Deep down, I think many of us have a sneaking suspicion that it can't be true that college from 18 to 21-ish is the secret to success. Signs everywhere show us the world is evolving beyond our previous guidebooks' paths for where to go and what to do to succeed. College right after high school may be a great goal for you, but it's not the *only* way forward.

We're going to have to dig a little deeper now to find our way — away from what "experts" who don't know our unique strengths, talents, and circumstances tell us is right. They can open our minds and perspectives, but we will need to also include our own insights created from taking care of our beautiful selves and authentic connection with others. You probably keep witnessing the failures of the old ways of doing things and are having a hard time buying into traditional ways of going about success.

We know of too many people who have created a great life for themselves without 4.0s. We also know too many stories of the people who went on that track and ended up miserable. So, what if that's not the goal?

When I let my mind wander about it, I think that we're more motivated by happiness than what others tell us we should do to be successful. We can get ourselves to do stuff that can be difficult and challenging because it feels good to enrich our minds. When we build more connections between neurons, the world becomes more interesting and less a source of confusion and fear. We learn to wonder, ask questions, and search for meaning. We start to wire in the neurochemicals that produce satisfaction from problem-solving. It feels good to solve a puzzle, work out a complicated problem, or come to a conclusion about a complicated question. We can have satisfaction, creativity, and meaningful connection as goals that motivate our actions, too.

Poet (and my personal rock star) Mary Oliver once said that attention without feeling is only a report. Do we want to create lives that look like a report? What if an adventure story or a sweet, moving poem might make us happier? I think adults tend to steer kids towards the report because it's safe, and we worry the only other alternative could be a horror story.

But it's not. I bet you were more drawn to the word happy in the title than the word grades. So before moving on, take a deep breath and name the feeling you wish to have more of as a result of reading *The Happy Grades Workbook*.

How To Use This Workbook

If you get bored with study strategies, don't worry! I do too, but I've learned them all. I've tested them all out with hundreds of kids over my 20+ years as a teacher and learning specialist, and I'm only including the ones I know work the best and are the least boring to implement.

I'm also sprinkling them with some magic fairy dust that makes everything less boring and a lot more enjoyable: the art and science of creativity and happiness. If that sounds interesting to you, then hooray! You have found your guide. There's a reason this is in your hands right now.

If that sounds like a load of crap to you, you have a choice:

1. Scan over this and see if anything catches your eye that might be useful, or
2. Don't give this another minute and go find something else on school skills you like better

There's a ton of good stuff out there on ways to be successful, so I am sure you'll find one that works for you.

The sections from here on out are filled with activities you can try out right away. I've done my best to make things visual and chunked it into easy-to-take steps. You'll see this later in the book, but treat each strategy like an experiment. Find one you think will help you feel better about an area of your life and give it a good try for at least a week.

Here are a few possible ways to use this book:

- Check out the table of contents and go right to the part you think will help you the most right now.

- Read it all the way through from start to finish and put a Post-it note next to the parts you want to go back to try.
- Open it up randomly to a page and adopt that page for one day. Try it out. Make connections from what you're seeing around you to what you read. Share something you found interesting with someone else.
- Flip through and stop when you hit a page that catches your eye — maybe it's the way it's laid out or a word you spot that catches your attention. Start there. Read it. Try it out. See how that goes for you. Then, when you feel like you need another boost, flip through it again.

The habit tracker below is a good place to keep track of the things that are working for you that you want to keep going with.

> **You can find extra habit trackers in the templates at the end of the workbook.**
>
> **Visit h2c.ai/hgw to download more book bonuses.**

HABIT	1	2	3	4	5	6	7

As you read through the strategies in the book, add the ones that seem interesting to you to this list. You can either take this page out, print one out from the book bonuses download page, or just make your own on a note card. A great way to make habits stick is to use a tracker like this one. Choose about three habits you think would make your life work better. Keep the list by your bed (or some other place where you will notice it every day) and check off whether or not you followed through with it each day. No worries if you didn't. It's just information, and checking it daily helps you keep it top of mind. Make a new one at the end of the week and see if you can do a little better collecting more check marks the next week. We're going to learn a lot more about habits in the next section.

SECTION 1:
GET PEACEFUL

- On a scale of 1-5, how would you rate the clutter factor in these different areas of your life?
  - 1 = Free, clear, and open like the fresh blue sky on a crisp spring day.
  - 5 = Crowded like the stuffed, slightly sour-smelling dark pockets of my son's backpack.

1-5	AREA OF MY LIFE	1-5	AREA OF MY LIFE
	My mind		My school stuff
	My schedule		My workspace

	IN THIS SECTION, YOU'LL LEARN ABOUT:
1	**Building and sticking with meaningful habits**
	Keep them small
	Keep them meaningful
	Keep them visible
2	**Decluttering**
	Your mind through brain dumps and journaling, turning around automatic negative thoughts, and mindfulness
	Your stuff through all-in-one systems and overhauls
	Your time by unscheduling it and making it visible

P.S. Making a prediction about what you're about to read (what the author is going to sound like and what it's going to be about) is a great way to increase focus while you read. It's natural to want to see if you're right or not. So while you read, you'll be looking out for information to either prove or disprove your prediction, which is better than just sitting there letting it all go in one neuron and out the other.

P.P.S. I can't be sure, but I'm almost positive that information going into a neuron and out of another one is *not* the scientifically accurate way to describe reading.

Get Peaceful Pep Talk

Last week, my 12-year-old son slept through his alarm on a Monday morning. When I realized he still wasn't up with 30 minutes left before he had to leave for school, I woke him up by letting the dog run in and lick his face. He rolled away from the dog, putting him face to face with the clock. His first words to greet the new week were:

"I am dead."

This could possibly be one of the worst thoughts to have if your goal is to have a happy and peaceful day.

I found out later that the reason for his dread on top of being late was that he had decided to put off his weekend homework and do it before school on Monday. Having a track record of exactly zero times that he was able to do this before, it wasn't a solid plan.

You see, getting peaceful is about more than meditating and taking nature walks (although that definitely helps, and I highly recommend it). You'll have a lot less stress in your life if you design it with peace in mind.

How Getting More Peaceful Helps You

Each of the suggestions on these pages gives you ways to design your life for more peace. With more peace, you will find that the hard stuff feels less hard. You free your mind up to think about more interesting and complex ideas, because you aren't bogged down strategizing how to get out of the panic and despair caused by reacting to the latest catastrophe — like sleeping through your alarm and not having your homework done. When things are good, you'll enjoy it more. And you'll use that energy to bounce back when things aren't so good.

Even if you don't care about school so much, I bet you care about being a good friend, family member, or neighbor to other people. Creating the conditions for inner peace makes it so much more likely that you'll be at your best and able to help others. So even if school isn't your first priority, you can use your sense of purpose to be someone others can rely on to make some of these changes. Coincidentally, it'll most likely improve some things at school, too. It's sort of the wonderful way this all works.

When you feel better, you start to do better for yourself and others. Getting peaceful is one of the key ways I have found that makes me feel and do better.

On the other end of the spectrum from my story about my son are kids like Jenna. While she was in 10th grade, she told me that she was sacrificing sleep to study, write, and recopy notes, so that she could get all As. Even though it was exhausting for her, it would be worth it by the winter break, because she'd ace her finals and then get to rest.

The challenge, my dear Jennas out there, is that there will always be the next big push.

> **Don't push peace off for some time in the future when you've finally made it to get to relax.**

You can build simple systems and habits that help you to relax now and in the future. If you push super hard so that you can have peace later, then you'll find that you're too exhausted to actually enjoy it.

Check one of these statements that best describes you:	
	I tend to put off tasks that could be hard or boring until the last minute.
	I tend to burn myself out doing tasks that feel hard and boring, so I can enjoy myself at some later date.
	I go back and forth between those and haven't quite found a balance yet.
	I've got this peaceful balance thing figured out!

Go through these activities and pick up the ones that resonate with you. Not all of these will be for everyone at the moment it's read. Some might be better for different times in your life.

Except for this first one: habits.

Building (and Sticking with) Meaningful Habits

Habits are the magic fairy dust that turn any of these strategies from being just plain information into positive, happy change for you. So that's where we begin.

Habits are the superstar of the self-improvement world for a good reason. A habit is an action, thought, or feeling that you repeat so many times it becomes something you do, think, or feel without even trying. They're powerful. You have habits whether you try to create them or not. This is great if it's something that creates more health, wellness, happiness, and peace in your life. Those habits could be brushing your teeth before bed, hugging a loved one when you get in the door from a long day, or throwing your arms open when you get out of bed in the morning and declaring, "What a beautiful day!"

However, habits can have a dark side, too. That can be listening to the voice that says, "That can wait," or only rereading notes the night before the test, even though that didn't work the last three times you "studied" for a test.

There's a reason I'm putting habits front and center in the section about getting peaceful. It's because habits clear our minds from having to make a gazillion mundane decisions about how to be the person you most want to be.

> "Habits are the body's way of lightening the load on our brains, of putting problem-solving on autopilot in order to free up room to take in more information and perform more tasks" (Sincero 2020).

I fully agree with Jen Sincero. I would also suggest that we don't take on habits for the purpose of taking in more information anwd performing more tasks. Instead, we free up some cognitive space to get some light and peace in there.

Ready to start building habits that help you get peaceful?

What's a Habit?

A habit is an action you do all the time, so you barely think about it. Brushing your teeth, hugging your mom or dad when you walk into the kitchen in the morning, and saying thanks to your teacher on your way out the door at the end of class are all habits. (Okay, those are shameless plugs for things that warm my heart, but hopefully they will give you some ideas.) Habits can help us move in the direction we want to go in, or habits can get in our way. So, our first step is to just take a good, clear look at your habits as they are right now.

What Makes a Habit Effective?

Effective habits — even ones that help you raise your grades — are so much easier to develop and stick to when they're about becoming the type of person you want to be, rather than tied to an outcome you want to get, like good grades or lots of money. There's nothing wrong with good grades and lots of money, and I truly wish all of that for you. However, research shows that attaching your habits to a goal about an external reward like that rather than an internal identity just doesn't stick with you for the long haul (like over the course of a semester or year). For that, it's better to fit your habits to the type of person you would feel happy and proud to be. So, we'll also be taking a look at the type of person you want to be and upgrading your current habits with that in mind.

Notice I'm not using the words good or bad to describe your habits. That's because, in the words of James Clear:

> "The labels 'good habit' and 'bad habit' are slightly inaccurate. There are no good habits or bad habits. There are only effective habits. That is, effective at solving problems. All habits serve you in some way — even the bad ones — which is why you repeat them" (Clear 2018).

It's useful to think about that for a minute. What problems are your bad habits helping you to solve? Getting clear on that will help you figure out a better solution.

What Makes a Habit Sticky?

You probably have had ideas, maybe even made heroic efforts before, about how to change your ways and "be better." And I'm sure you've also experienced the way life gets in the way of all those great ideas and intentions. Our brain's love for keeping things the same means it's even harder to break old patterns, even the ones you know rationally aren't working so well. Also, as we all know now for real, there are a lot of external events out of our control. It happens in big ways, like COVID-19, and small ways, like a teacher assigning something on a Wednesday when you already made plans for the week that didn't include spending an hour reading an article for class the next day.

So no offense to you or the other people in your life, but you really shouldn't rely on your brain or others to magically power over your impulse control when it comes time to make a different kind of choice of sticking with a new habit. Eventually, over time and with practice, your new habit will be on repeat, so you won't even need to think about it. For a little while though, you'll need to rely on some other methods to keep it going. The best one I know of is to make your new habit visible. That will be our last exercise to get all this good work to stick and make some positive changes in your life.

Exercise 1: Look at Your Current Habits

This exercise is about reviewing your current habits. It's useful to check in with yourself from time to time about what habits have become part of your daily life. In the next exercise, we'll look at ways to change your habits.

This method has been adapted from James Clear's super popular book, *Atomic Habits*. If you have the time, read it! But, in the meantime, do this.

Method

1. Review your habits.
2. Turn off your self-criticism.
3. Think about what kind of habits they are.
4. Note down the kind of habits they are.

Review Your Habits

Go through your whole day from start to finish and list out any habits that come to mind. Try to get at least five listed on the scorecard below.

Note: not all habits are positive ones. For example, I have a very annoying habit of eating crackers while I make dinner as if they're my actual dinner. Be sure to list the ineffective ones here, too. So just imagine yourself going through your day from morning until nighttime. Write down whatever behaviors you seem to do on repeat without even thinking that either help you towards the type of person you want to be or aren't doing you any favors in that department.

MY CURRENT HABITS	+ / -
Morning	
Lunchtime	
After School	
Bedtime	

Turn Off Your Self-Criticism

Okay, now breathe. That could have been hard for you. Chances are this activity made you look at some not-so-effective habits. Try your best, just for now while you do the exercises in this book, to put your little self-critical and judge-y inner troll aside. You can pick it back up if you really want it around later. But the troll's going to make it harder for you, and I want this to feel as easy and delightful as possible.

Think about What Kind of Habits They Are

So now you should have at least five habits that either help you to feel good and powerful or aren't contributing much to the quality of your life. The next step is evaluating them so it's clear what's working for you and what you want to change.

Note Down the Kind of Habits They Are

Finally, go through the list and write a plus sign or minus sign next to each one to show if it's effective (+) or ineffective (−).

Exercise 2: Visualize Your Happy Habits

Habits that will make you happier and more successful need to have some deeper meaning to you than just a bunch of actions other people say you should do to be a good student. Follow the steps below to come up with some ideas to upgrade your habit scorecard. Include habits that are about the type of person you want to be, rather than the outcome you want to get.

Method

1. Brainstorm words to describe the type of person you want to be.
2. Imagine the habits of that type of person.
3. Play the Copy/Edit/Delete Game with your habit scorecard.

Brainstorm Words to Describe the Person You Want to Be

If you're not sure, you can also start in the other direction. What are some words to describe the type of person you don't want to be?

> **For a list of "being words" that have worked for past students for inspiration, check out the book bonuses here: h2c.ai/hgw**

If you went with the "don't want to be" direction, google the opposites of those words and replace them with their happier, more positive counterparts that make you feel good.

Imagine that Person's Habits

Imagine a person who has those qualities, either real or imaginary. Go ahead and give them a name. I worked with a teacher once named Janice who I admired for how she took care of her responsibilities and managed to be quite cheerful and relaxed about it all, too. Fill out the habit scorecard as they would. What does "Janice" do on repeat that you imagine helps her be that way? Try to write at least five daily habits on your imaginary person's habit scorecard.

> **Bonus: Add a few thoughts this person repeatedly thinks in certain situations that help them follow through with the habits on their scorecard. Thoughts can be habits too!**

	_____'S HABITS	+ / -
Morning		
Lunchtime		
After School		
Bedtime		

Play the Copy/Edit/Delete Game with Your Scorecard

Take your original scorecard that shows your current habits. Now let's play the Copy/Edit/Delete Game. Consider the ways you might make your scorecard just a little bit more like the person you want to be.

- What's one habit you'd like to delete from your scorecard? Go ahead and cross it out.
- What's one habit you'd like to copy and paste from the imaginary person's scorecard that you think would make a big difference in your life right now? Add that one to your habit scorecard and make it stand out.
- Finally, what's one habit on your or the imaginary person's scorecard that you can edit by making a small change to it to make it more effective or easier to repeat more often? Add or edit that one on your habit scorecard.

Exercise 3: Make Your Habit Change Visible

Now for the fun, creative part. This will help you remember to follow through on your habits daily.

Method

1. Decide on just one change you want to make with a proclamation.
2. Make your habit change visible.

Decide with a Proclamation

Making a proclamation helps officially make your decisions about how you want to be and act. It also helps to be clear about the deeper, more meaningful reason behind the decision. Use the proclamation below to take this first step.

On this date_____ (add date here), I have made the decision

to_____ (add habit

you've decided to edit, copy, or delete from your habit scorecard)

so that I can _____

_____ (add the effect you hope

for this to have on improving the quality of your life, being the type

of person you want to be, or whatever positive outcome you want to

create for yourself with it).

Signed,

_____

Example proclamations from past students:

- On this date, I'm making the decision to make a Quizlet right after finishing my science notes for homework, so that I study them earlier and more often and raise my grade, which will make me feel more effective and happy.
- On this date, I'm making the decision to go for a 15-minute jog as soon as I get home from school, so that I can be more energetic and focused in the afternoons.
- On this date, I'm making the decision to clean out and organize my binder and backpack every Friday after school, so that I can be more clear and less stressed about having what I need and knowing what I need to do.

Make Your Habit Change Visible

Remember how we talked about making your habit "sticky"? Since you can't rely on just your brain to make a new habit stick, making the change visible can help you practice putting your habit on repeat until you don't really have to think about it.

Take a look at this list of ideas to make your habit change visible. Choose one of the methods below or come up with your own.

- Write your new habit change down in at least three different places you'll see all the time. Get clever with it. Write it with a dry erase marker on your bathroom mirror, so it greets you every time you check yourself out. Stick it on a note that you put in your underwear drawer, so you have to push it out of the way and think of it when you reach in there (hopefully every day). Set it up as a repeating reminder on your phone or computer at a prime time each day. The point is to get that thing in front of your eyeballs as much as possible.

- Attach the new habit to something you already do every day. One of my students wanted to start taking his ADHD medication every day. He put the bottle on the shelf with the cereal he ate every morning and attached it to his breakfast routine. A good formula to use for this strategy is: "When I (thing you do already), I will (new habit you want to start)." Want to start checking your work regularly before handing in your tests? Try: "When I write my name on the test, I will write 'Breathe! Check your work.' at the bottom to remind me to check my work when I get to the end."

- For at least the first one to three weeks while you work on becoming cozy with a new habit, wear a string around your wrist. Every time you feel it there or see it, take a moment, and visualize yourself doing the new habit. Alternatively, you can throw something new and weird you're not used to seeing into your usual environment. Every time you see it there, visualize yourself doing the new habit and your reason for doing it. One of my students put their old, pink My Little Pony on top of their dresser to help them remember their intention to get started on their research project before getting into anything else after they got home from school.

- Get a jar and a bag of fun colorful pom-poms from the craft section of the store. Every time you successfully do your new habit, add a puff ball to the jar. Now, I find it fun and satisfying to see puff balls pile up in a jar. If you need some extra incentive, you can reward yourself with something fun to do or get if you fill the jar (or negotiate with a parent for it).

- Add the new habit to your habit tracker that you have right next to your bed. Before you get into bed, give yourself a sticker, smiley face, or a good old-fashioned check mark every time you repeat the habit.

Happy Grades

Which strategy will you use to make your new habit visible?

To remember this new habit, I can . . .

Many of my students have trouble "remembering to remember" things. Any of those visibility strategies will also work for anything you want to make a point to remember.

22

Decluttering Your Stuff and Your Mind

I wish there was a snazzier word for decluttering. Trust me, it can be so much more fun and inspiring than it sounds. To me, decluttering is about appreciating what makes you happy and getting rid of all the other stuff that makes it too crowded to see and have more of what makes you happy.

But I want to warn you. When I talk about decluttering, I'm not talking about making everything look cute and perfect and worthy of some viral life-hack video. I see many students who go too far down that rabbit hole of decluttering and organizing as a form of procrastination. They never actually get anything that's lurking in their perfectly color-coded binders and to-do lists done.

Even Marie Kondo, the international sensation and icon of magical, minimalist, decluttered spaces, has recently admitted that she has "kind of given up" on keeping things tidy. Instead, she's investing in clearing the clutter in the mental and emotional spaces that can really make our life feel heavier and more difficult than it needs to be. To help with that, we're going to include self-compassion in the decluttering process. Self-compassion is an attitude that involves treating yourself with kindness and understanding in difficult times. It recognizes that making mistakes is just part of being human. It's related to all sorts of positive benefits like higher grades, better relationships, and improved productivity. But I like it because it just makes me feel better, especially when things are harder than normal.

So, first and foremost, we take on decluttering with the purpose of clearing our minds and emotions to be able to think clearly and feel better. Having a physical space to work and rest that doesn't make you think, "This is gross, and I hate being here," does help with all that.

The Magic and Neuroscience of Imagination

To help you declutter your physical space, especially if you don't identify as the neat and organized type, we're going to take advantage of the power of your imagination again to visualize a more organized, ideal space. The magical thing is that just being able to imagine your space decluttered will make you naturally start working to make it look that way. You will start to see easy and creative solutions to keep up with it. It's not actually magic. It's neuroscience.

The reticular activating system (RAS) is a cluster of cells in the brain that processes new incoming information and controls our awareness, so we can act in certain ways to keep our beliefs and identities nice and safe. If your brain's RAS sees your intention regularly, it will start focusing your attention on the actions and resources available to make that happen. It's like when my son went through his sneaker obsession phase and pined after a very specific pair of sneakers. He not only started seeing them everywhere, but also started seeing more opportunities to work odd jobs to make the money to afford them.

What Does Decluttering Have to Do with Time Management?

Most of my clients tell me that they think they should get better at time management. When we dig into that, past the layers of what everyone has told them they need improve, they usually realize that getting a better grip on how they handle time will help them be less stressed. Because I believe that everyone deserves to live in peace, and I'm on a mission to use my own weird talents to make that possible for more people, and I am not naturally gifted at time management myself, I set out to learn and test as many methods as I could.

Essential Principles of Time Management

I have learned some key things about time management:

- There are as many good systems for managing time as there are humans, so focus less on picking the "right" one and focus more on just having one.
- It's okay to change up your system to keep it fresh and continuously working for you during different seasons in your year and life. I find many of my students with ADHD (and yours truly) do better when they change their system every few months. The novelty can help if you need a little extra boost of dopamine to pay attention to something that has become routine.
- Time is a pretty trippy concept. For one thing, there isn't a single part of your brain or body that keeps track of time. It truly is more of a feeling than a scientific fact. For another thing, when you're a teenager, your time awareness is still in development. You really don't have a reliable sense for judging how much time something might take or even how much time is passing. For those reasons, you need to have a system that makes that invisible, trippy concept of time into a visible, concrete thing you can move around — preferably by hand, so you feel physically more in control of it.
- No matter what, just make your time visible and put the stuff you need to get done outside of your head and somewhere you can see it. It's literally creating time with your own two hands. You can channel your inner Chronos, the mythical Greek god who controlled time. He ended up being pretty destructive with that power, but I know you'll use it with much more good in mind, right?

What Should I Declutter from My Mind?

Psychologists have identified two types of mind clutter that really get in our way: worry and rumination. Worry is usually defined by thoughts about our future. Many of my students try to keep a lot in their heads of what they have to do, remember, and follow through on. It's like they have a whole bunch of worry tabs open on their phones they don't even see, running their battery down and slowing their efforts.

The place where they store that is an area called *working memory*. This is an area of your brain that's like a whiteboard with an annoying quirk. It has disappearing ink and nothing you write on it stays on it for very long without rewriting it over again. So unless you keep reminding yourself in your head that you should start the paper or finish the test corrections on Wednesday, you will forget until you check your school's portal to find out that all of that is due on the same day, and that day starts in about eight hours.

And, if by chance you do rewrite that information over and over again in your mind whiteboard, it has another quirk I haven't mentioned yet. The whiteboard is pretty small. It only has space for a very limited amount of information. So if you're rewriting your tasks in your head, you're crowding out space you could be using for much more useful information you need to apply sooner, like the chemistry formula you studied two nights ago for the quiz you're taking right now, or that it's your best friend's birthday, and you want to bring them a cupcake at lunch.

Now let's get into the other kind of mind clutter I mentioned: rumination. Instead of thoughts about the future, rumination tends to get stuck in the past. Negative self-talk is a form of rumination that takes an uncomfortable, unpleasant, or traumatic circumstance from our past and tries to get us to avoid it. It does this by saying pretty mean things about ourselves to keep us from getting into that situation again. Psychologists even have a cute name for it because it's so common: *Automatic Negative Thoughts*, or ANTs for short. These are repetitive thoughts that we tend to use against ourselves for a good reason. Deep down we think that if we talk to ourselves like a mean drill sergeant, we'll kick it into gear and avoid mistakes. Our ANTs mean well, but they aren't all that helpful in the long run.

So, decluttering is a whole heart, mind, and hands endeavor. Don't worry if that sounds over-whelming, because I'm going to break it down for you in simple, even enjoyable steps. So students can be more peaceful and therefore happier and more successful, we tackle decluttering on three levels: physical stuff, time, and their minds. Let's start with stuff.

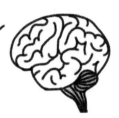

Exercise 1: Declutter Your Stuff

I'm sure you have some spaces in your life that you often interact with that could use a declutter-ified upgrade. Maybe you waste precious time and energy trying to find something in a messy backpack. Maybe it's hard to feel good drifting off to sleep in a room that makes you feel claustrophobic and stressed. Let's clear those, so you can feel better and create more energy and space for doing better, too.

Method

1. Identify one space to declutter that makes you feel stressed, heavy, or just plain icky when you think about it or see it.
2. Apply self-compassion.
3. Design it.
4. Apply microbursts.

Identify One Space to Declutter

Think about all the physical spaces you interact with the most that are in your control. There are some examples below. Put a check mark next to just one that makes you feel kind of stressed, tired, cringey, or gross when you think of or look at it.

WHAT PHYSICAL SPACES MAKE ME STRESSED?	
Clothes closet	Backpack
Drawers	Binder or folders for school
Desk area	Digital folders
Nightstand	Other:
Locker	Other:

Notice that I didn't say to mark one that's cluttered. Sometimes clutter can be inspiring when you're in the middle of a project. My workspace is full of stacks of books that inspire me and Post-its with mottos written on them that help me remember the type of person I want to be. I like the way it feels to work surrounded by words that inspire me. However, if my project management systems and to-do lists gets too full and disorganized, I can't think straight.

Apply Self-Compassion

Take a deep breath in and out. When you breathe out, send yourself some love, even if that feels weird or silly. It might be, but it helps. It might help to put your hand over your heart when taking a couple deep breaths. I suggest this because tackling an area that's cluttered and stressful can make you feel sort of ashamed about it and want to avoid it altogether. It's totally okay! Lots of accomplished, incredible, good, and successful people aren't naturally organized. You're in good company.

Design It

Below, sketch what it would look like if the area you chose was in its best, most decluttered, glow-iest state. This doesn't have to be a professional-designer-looking sketch, or totally clear and minimalist (but if you're into that kind of thing, then go for it). Just draw blobs, circles, and rectangles, if that's the extent of your drawing ability, to represent the things you most want and need in that space for it to function well for you. Add labels to the important details in your picture and write what goes where.

Give the stuff you need on hand the most a dedicated home.

Here's a picture of my peaceful, decluttered _____.

Stick your picture up in the area you wish to look that way and let that RAS I mentioned earlier work its magic.

Apply Microbursts

Microbursts are short, deliberate, and focused periods of working on something. Put on a timer for 10 minutes with some peppy music (or your favorite music) and do a microburst of decluttering. See how much you can do in that time to get it closer to your picture. Do this again about once a week or more if you want to. When it's looking good, you can repeat this exercise with another one of the areas on your list.

> "We have the power, now, today, to keep only things that bring us joy in our lives. Make sure you are doing this with your physical space. While stuff can't make you happy, if you surround yourself with objects you are crazy about and then invest care into those objects, you can increase the overall enchantment you feel in your life" (Schuster 2020).

Exercise 2: Declutter Your Time

This is typically the place in a traditional school skills workbook where we'd get into using some form of planner. I really enjoy a good planning system, but don't worry if you've not yet been able to keep up with a planner. This is all about energy management instead of time management, so this exercise is going to be about creating the time for the things that help you restore your energy and feel like you're enjoying this time in your life, not just planning it all away on stuff you'd really rather not be doing.

Methods

Here are three methods you can use to declutter your time:

1. Make your time visible.
2. Unschedule your time.
3. Declutter time wasters.

Method 1: Make Your Time Visible

Making your time visible means just what it sounds like — writing out how you spend your time (or need to spend it) in a way you can see. If you want to use a planner, go for it, but if you hate using planners, this can be done with a blank piece of paper, too. In fact, that's what most of my students do. You can also use the template included in the book bonuses. Whatever you use, stick the paper somewhere you'll see it all the time. Do this once a week. Most of my students like to do this on Sunday or Monday evening.

Follow these steps to make sure you include all the important stuff:

1. Put in all your due dates, big events, and meetings, and highlight them so they stand out. If using a digital planner, I suggest creating these as events.
2. Now that you can see what needs your time and attention all in one place, you can plan backward from there. How do you want to approach getting ready for each of those items? What steps do you want to take? How far in advance do you need to take them to feel like you are prepared in accordance with the type of person you want to be?

3. Remember to look ahead to what's coming up after the weekend. This accounts for any early-in-the-week surprises and things in the future you want to keep on the radar. It also stops any nagging feelings taking up space in your energy and mind that there might be surprises that you won't be ready for.

You can see an example of this below.

Simple Time Manager

2. Break your due dates into steps and spread them out so you aren't overwhelmed the night before.

1. Put in all your due dates and highlight them to make them stand out.

M	T
Homework: – Spanish lesson – Make Science flash cards – 1/2 of History paper	Volleyball Chapter 5 Spanish Quiz **Homework:** – Finish History paper – Practice Science flash cards
W History paper due **Homework:** – Science study group – English journal due Friday	**Th** Band practice Science Test! **Homework:** – Math pages 27-28, exercises 1-22a, 26-30
F Aboretum Permission Slip English jounral entry due Turn in Math homework	**Sa/Su** **Homework:** – Outline Science lab – Math practice test

Next Week
Science lab > Tuesday
Math Test > Wednesday

3. Look ahead to see what's coming up after the weekend so you can get ready for it.

For some more suggestions and support, you can find recommendations for best planners and information about time management by checking out my blog, subscribing to my newsletter, and accessing free resources at triciaunderwood.com

Method 2: Unschedule Your Time

Another way to declutter your time is something called *unscheduling*. That's when you purposely block out time in your schedule each week to do something fun and relaxing. If you get that in your schedule first and then plan around it, your brain will know it has plenty of time for the things it wants to do, so it might go easier on you when you have to get some homework done.

Make a chart of things you want to dedicate time to that help you be a healthy, happy person. Estimate how much time you'll need for them.

THINGS THAT HELP ME FEEL HEALTHY AND HAPPY	TIME ESTIMATE
Exercise	3x/week for 30 minutes

Now schedule those activities into your plans. Do this by drawing boxes around time in your planner or creating an event for it in your digital planner.

Method 3: Declutter Time Wasters

It's super obvious, right? I've seen some pretty interesting changes happen when the only step a student takes to declutter their schedule is just clarifying what wastes their time.

For the next two days, keep a little note card in your pocket. Every time you catch yourself wasting time doing something that isn't adding a whole lot of value to the person you want to become, write down what you caught yourself doing.

The interesting thing is that both research and my own experience shows that just by being more aware of these time wasters, you start cutting down how much time you spend doing them. It leaves you with more of what you really want in this whole enterprise anyway: time for stuff that makes you feel happy, relaxed, and fulfilled.

Exercise 3: Declutter Your Mind

If you do nothing else in this section, this one will be worth the time and cost I put into getting this book in front of your eyeballs.

If you're making your time visible, you're already doing a lot to declutter your mind. But this step involves getting rid of those little thought gremlins I mentioned earlier called automatic negative thoughts (ANTs). If you have a thought that makes you feel bad about yourself, or makes you lose motivation to start something in your best interest for your success, then it's probably an ANT. Also, because I believe truth always feels freer and more open than a lie, there's probably a much better, truer thought you can believe instead.

Method:

1. Learn to spot them.
2. Don't fight with them or for them. Just observe them.
3. Look for evidence that they might not be true.
4. Create a turnaround thought.

Learn to Spot Them

Check the chart below to identify which ANTs might be cluttering your mind and taking up space you could be using for more interesting, relaxing, or happier things. Put a check mark next to any that look familiar.

EXAMPLE THOUGHT	YEP, I DO THIS
I'm failing math (after getting one bad quiz score when all your other grades are solidly above a failing level).	
The teacher is going to be mad at me.	
When you have a good outcome, you tend to think it was just a fluke or luck, but when something bad happens, you think it's because there's something wrong with you. I'm not good enough, so I'll probably do this wrong.	
I'm probably never getting into college.	
I should be more [insert adjective].	
I'm a bad test-taker.	
Other people have this figured out, so something must be wrong with me.	

What are three of your most common ANTs? What do your ANTs say when they are cluttering up your mind and making it hard for you to do things that can make you happier and more successful in school and life? Next to each one, note the situation that usually triggers the thought. This is usually a place, person, or activity.

MY ANTS	TRIGGERING SITUATION

Don't Fight with Them or for Them

Fighting *with* ANTs sounds like: "I shouldn't think that! Stop thinking that way! I'm only making it worse! Think more positively!"

Fighting *for* your ANTs sounds like: "I'm just a bad test taker, so that's how it is. There's really nothing I can do. I'm just bad at math."

Instead, just take a breath in and observe them like you're a little kid watching ants marching in a line across the sidewalk. Interesting! Look at them doing all their ant stuff.

> **Ask yourself: How would I feel or act differently if I didn't believe this thought?**

Look for Evidence That It Might Not Be True

Release what you don't want. Take a deep breath. As you breathe out, wonder: is there any way at all that this could not be true? List some reasons that explain why any of the ants you identified above might not be 100 percent true below.

WAYS MY ANT(S) MIGHT NOT BE TRUE	
1	
2	
3	

If you're really stuck, here's some evidence that rings true for many of my students that might also help you.

- I've been through hard things before and came out okay.
- I am a great friend, and I'm a good person.
- I have some people around me who I can go to for support if I need help.

Shining some light on evidence that contradicts the thoughts will make the ANTs shrivel up into a dry pile of ashes that blows away in the breeze like a vampire getting too much sun.

Create a Turnaround Thought

Create a new phrase that still rings true but is more aligned with how you really want to be. Martha Beck calls this a *turnaround thought*, and she is Oprah's life coach, so I'm going to do what she says.

Basically, twist and turn that ANT around in different ways until you get to a thought that makes you feel lighter, more positive, and more hopeful. You could try:

- Stating the exact opposite
- Moving and changing the verbs around
- Adding a "yet" or "possible" in there

Here are some examples for inspiration, and to show you that it might take a few tries before you find one that's true.

ANT: DOING HOMEWORK IS GOING TO BE DREADFUL	
1	**It's dreadful not to do homework.** I don't believe this one. It feels like I'm lying to myself.
2	**Not doing homework is going to be dreadful.** This one is sort of true to me. It has potential.
3	**Doing homework is going to be dread-less.** This one feels the best because it makes me start thinking of ways I can do homework to make it less dreadful, like maybe doing it with a friend, sitting outside, putting music on, taking breaks every 20 minutes to hang out with my dog, feeling really good after I get it done, etc.

ANT: I'M TERRIBLE AT TAKING TESTS	
1	Try the opposite: **I am great at taking tests.** Well, that doesn't feel so true to me, so I'll keep going.

ANT: I'M TERRIBLE AT TAKING TESTS

2	Try flipping the words around: **Tests are terrible at taking me.** I think I'm onto something here.
3	Try tweaking the words: **Tests are terrible at taking me down.** This one feels good. Like I am more than just taking a test. I can do more about it. Save my grade using other strengths. Maybe get some help and get better at tests anyway. I am not going to let a test take me down. I am so much more than that.

Bonus Strategies

Here's two more quick and simple methods to declutter your mind: meditation and brain dumps.

Meditation

Even just five minutes a day can help. You can DIY it by just closing your eyes and noticing your breath for five minutes. Or you could start with guided meditations. Your mind will wander, and you'll lose your attention. Once you notice that it has strayed, know that it's working! Now you can gently bring your attention back to noticing your breath.

> **You can find my favorite resources for guided meditations by going to the book bonuses: h2c.ai/hgw**
>
> **I also teach mindfulness-based stress reduction techniques specifically for teenage and young adult students. You can find information about when I'm offering that training by subscribing to my newsletter or contacting me through my website at triciaunderwood.com**

Brain Dumps

Before starting on a task where you'll need focus, or really any time your mind starts to feel cluttered with worry or stress, dump it all out on a page. Set a timer for five minutes and write it out.

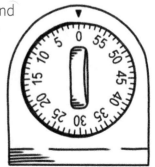

When you see it out of your mind and on a page, it literally takes up less space in your head. Suddenly, it looks a lot smaller and more controllable. Doing this for just one minute before a test is said to decrease test-taking anxiety and increase test performance. It's also a good thing to do for one minute before you start homework to increase focus.

Section 1 Reflection

Take a moment to fill out this chart. Use it to sort out your thoughts on the section and make them useful.

What are the main ideas or points that seem important to you?	Why is something you read about particularly important or relevant to you?
When might you use something you learned?	**Who could you reach out to for help? Can you think of anyone you could help with something you learned?**

P.S. Taking five minutes to fill out a what, who, when, why chart at the end of any section you've read for school is a quick way to make what you read stick. You can always substitute a different question to fit the reading, such as: What were the main points? Who were the most important people involved? When did the important things take place? Why does it matter?

Peace is important, but now we get to turn up the fun. In the next section, we wake up your ability to play that often gets put to sleep when it comes to school and academics. Getting playful helps make the things you have to do and remember for school a lot easier. Good news, it's something you've known how to do since you were a baby, so it really isn't all that hard. Read on to learn how you can easily add in the element of play to increase success and happiness at school.

GET PEACEFUL KEY TAKEAWAYS	
Keep habits small. Make them meaningful and visible.	
1	Remove the "should" from habits — make them more about you and who you want to be than what other people say you "should" be doing.
2	Declutter the space around you.
3	Make time management more about energy management by making time visible and unscheduling it to include things that you make you a happy and healthy person.
4	Declutter automatic negative thoughts from your mind.

SECTION 2: GET PLAYFUL

- Have you ever made yourself feel worse about a situation by making it a much bigger deal than it needed to be?
- When you procrastinate with schoolwork, are you are avoiding it out of fear of not being good at it or the fear of it being boring?
- What would be different in your life if you were unavailable for boredom?

You might not even be able to imagine a life in which you can answer that last question and be successful at school at the same time. If that's the case, this section is especially for you.

	IN THIS SECTION, YOU'LL LEARN ABOUT:	
1	**How to avoid making problems worse**	
	Get playful with procrastination	
	Celebrate small wins	
	Develop a curiosity habit	
2	**How to be unavailable for boredom**	
	Gamify the boring stuff	
	Embrace novelty	
	Use fake till you make it for actions, but not emotions	

Get Playful Pep Talk

Yes, I did have electricity when I was in high school, but no, I did not have the internet. If I did have the internet, I probably would've found a dozen other ways to entertain myself on the evening I found myself about 12 hours away from the due date of my paper on Dante's "Inferno" in my junior year of high school.

Since I had exhausted all my usual procrastination strategies, I called my best friend, who was a freshman in college, for some stress relief and a pointer or two. I didn't always put papers off, but I had no ideas for this one. To me, the epic poem was a dense read about a man who has to travel through different levels of hell to find out in the end that everything means nothing. Fun!

I now have a much greater appreciation of the wild, creative path to enlightenment Dante created, but, at 15, I wasn't that deep. Instead I was anxious and angry that I didn't understand something that was supposed to be profound.

From the other end of my see-through, light-up, landline phone, my friend Erin started asking weird and ridiculous questions about it to make me laugh like, "But what kind of pants did he wear in that circle of hell?" We started joking about all the deep and usually depressing words that most of literature always seems to be about and yelled them out loud: Death! The end of innocence! The passing of time! I started saying whatever weird things came to mind about those things until I squawked, "Time is our best enemy."

We burst out laughing at that one, because what on Earth does that even mean? I had no idea, but someone needed the dorm phone, and it was getting too late to spend any more time brainstorming, so I went with it. I wrote a whole darn paper about some nonsense statement that flew out of my mouth and how it related to a story that I didn't understand. As it turned out, having to make some sense out of that idea and relate the poem to it helped me make something meaningful out of the whole thing. It must have struck a chord with my teacher because I got an A, partly because of my "originality of thought."

How to Prepare for Challenge with Play

So much of what you have to do in high school gets h e a v y. The stuff you have to learn about and the pressure to produce work when your mistakes are counted against you can feel like negative fun.

> "We're now running national education systems where mistakes are the worst thing you can make" (Robinson 2006).

I believe the best way to prepare yourself for the difficult things is to soak up all the peace, joy, fun, and light wherever you can.

The kid who walks into the PSAT their sophomore year seeing it for exactly what it is — a practice for a practice test for a test that is increasingly losing its relevance for one's success later in life — will take that practice test rested, without getting bogged down by extra stress. They'll be more likely to remember their experience. Maybe they'll remember which parts were easier than expected and which parts were weird or tricky. They might feel motivated to practice for those kinds of questions for the next time, rather than block the whole thing out like it was some sort of traumatic gauntlet they had to go through and never want to repeat again.

If you can't tell, I have opinions about some standardized tests, but let's go back to getting playful.

This section is filled with exercises to keep your perspective playful. When we play with experiences put in front of us, we relax more with them. We allow more of the goodness and fun to get into our systems. We also reduce the suffering caused by difficult things that come up in life.

> "We didn't know as children that we were creative. That we could keep creating, keep tinkering, and trust that something interesting would result if we just stuck with it" (Kelley 2013).

The first set of exercises will teach you how to clear the way for play. We do this by getting out of the habit of making challenges worse with misplaced fears and worries. The second set of exercises helps you lighten up the challenge of boredom with playful strategies. The good news is that there are some great ways to handle challenges that feel more like play than hard work. I know school already does a good job of giving you plenty of that!

Avoid Problem Pressing

I have found that life will bring the dark and difficult on its own without us needing to train and get tough for that experience. Extra-hard assignments or the threat of bad grades don't really have the intended results. The fear and stress involved may spur you into action in the short term. But in the long run, you'll have more energy to start challenging work when you feel lit up by curiosity, unburdened with the stress of messing up, and free to give something a try. You might already know this truth, and maybe you're lucky enough to have some teachers in your life who know it too.

In case you don't, however, this section will show you how to experiment with doing schoolwork with a creative and playful spirit. Creative people will often play with prototypes of their ideas when they work. A prototype is like a first draft. In her book *Break the Good Girl Myth*, Majo Molfino explains how she learned at Stanford University's famous design school that a prototype is a "small, easy-to-make version you can test without too much skin in the game." Whatever the big issue, possibly overwhelming change, or goal, we are going to learn how to shrink it down into a tiny version to play with to make it more fun and a lot less dreadful to tackle.

I know this is easier said than done. When everyone else's expectations, standards, and criticisms start merging with your own thoughts and feelings, they create an extra layer of pressure and fear about doing something wrong or not being good enough. I hear and feel those voices too, and I'm well out of school. But what I know for sure is that they get quieter when I make my work feel more like play.

How We Press on Problems to Make Them Hurt Even More

It's much easier to make schoolwork feel more like play if you learn how to make problems lighter. Mistakes, confusion, and performance pressure lift when we don't heap negative predictions, assumptions, and fears on top of them. It's like when a kid you're friendly with looks at you in a sort of weird way, you think they might hate you, when in reality, they were probably just a little gassy.

Making problems worse with extra fear and worry is a totally natural tendency that most of us do from time to time. We tend to try to protect ourselves from the pain of life by practicing for it. We can make things that don't have to be dark and difficult worse by loading up our brains with fears. We turn little bumps in the road into a huge, terrifying monster, so we move forward prepared for battle or stop in our tracks to avoid it altogether.

I call this problem pressing. It's like when you have a bruise, and you press on it to remind yourself that it's there.

Examples of Problem Pressing:

- When you miss a homework assignment and proceed to tell yourself that you are a total screwup who will never get their act together
- When you are confused about an assignment but think that it would sound stupid to ask about it, so you avoid it
- When you have a test coming up, you imagine all the things that could go wrong and the terrible consequences if you screw it up

So, this tendency has the very good intention of protecting us to make us stronger. The issue is that it doesn't actually help us out in the long term, and it feels awful.

How Getting Playful Helps

All that problem pressing, all that fear and worry, it can be a real motivation killer. A lack of motivation can be a big pain point for many of my students. Because motivation is created through action and not the other way around, we want to make these actions as easy to take as possible. We are much more likely to take action when it feels like play rather than pain.

In this section we're going to learn about curiosity, because we're a lot more motivated to get started on things we feel curious about. I think the first ingredient of curiosity is joy. For example, I find joy in looking at nature; reading fast-paced, wacky, and outlandish fiction books; and hanging out with people I find interesting and funny, and who I love (just to name a few). These show that I'm curious about beauty, art, and design, as well as off-beat, quirky, unexpected things, and humor. You'll have a chance in this section to identify some things you find naturally interesting, too.

It's fun to let your mind wander and wonder about stuff. It explains why the origin of the word scholastic is derived from the ancient Greek word *skholastikos*, meaning enjoying leisure and devoting one's leisure to learning. People learned as a leisure activity back then. They went to school just for the fun of it! It was a hobby reserved only for the most privileged. The people who had time to spend used it learning about why things work the way they do, how we came to be here, the nature of humanity, and the patterns in history and numbers. I guess at some point, probably when printing books became easier and cheaper, someone decided to organize it all and allow some commoners to learn a certain amount (they wanted to keep the social order in place). Now it can feel like school is filled with things that someone else says you have to learn to pass. Somewhere along the way, we lost our habit of being curious about things just because it's sort of fun to learn new things you didn't know about before.

Acting curious will make you seem sort of strange compared to the way others around you act. Some of the things I ask you to do in this section will have you feeling a little goofy. But guess what? Goofballs are fun! And having some fun allows for those feel-good chemicals I introduced you to earlier to start pumping through your system, so your brain subconsciously thinks, "Hey, that felt good. I'll get him to do that again next time." This is a great way to foster the feelings you need for motivation to happen more automatically.

I know deep down, or maybe right at the surface, you really care about being a good person who's happy and successful, and probably kind and helpful to others, too. You might even hope to solve some pretty big problems we all face in our world today. I think the best way to show you really care about those things is through curiosity, rather than stress and fear. Author of *Whole Brain Living*, Jill Bolte Taylor, says, "Curiosity is care, not worry." As a neuroanatomist at the top of her field who suffered a stroke that destroyed the entire analytical part of her brain that stored all her Harvard trained memories and information, she had quite a few things to worry about. It was curiosity, not worry that allowed her to essentially rebuild her brain so she could regain her physical, emotional, and thinking abilities. It can be hard to pose an open, curious question about something when you're feeling frustrated and worried about it. If you practice curiosity enough, it gets easier to remember when you're in the moment. Think, *what can I compare this to that's easier for me to understand? Who can I connect with that might be able to help? What's an easier way to start this? How can I make this better in some small ways first?*

> **P.S. Parents and educators, this goes for us and the students we care about, too.**

Exercise 1: Create a Sun-Beaming Wheel

You can avoid problem pressing on the things you have to do that are boring, difficult, or just not your strength at this moment by reminding yourself of ways to shrink it into a cute little prototype. I like to call it "sun-beaming it," because what you make in this exercise ends up looking like a sun with beams shooting out. The sun beams lighten up the task or goal you want to get done. Here's an example.

Method

1. Pick three activities you tend to procrastinate on.
2. Gather materials (paper and drawing utensils).
3. Draw a wheel with one of your procrastination activities on the inside and the spokes around it.
4. Fill the spokes with related actions that take no more than five minutes to complete.

Pick Three Activities You Tend to Procrastinate Doing

You probably don't need much help with this one. We all have them. Those things you put off into that mythical time of "later" when you will feel like doing it or hoping it will disappear. We both know 99 percent of the time, it doesn't quite work out that way.

Here's a list of the most common procrastination-causing activities for my students:

- Studying for a test
- Writing a paper
- Doing math homework
- Reading an assigned chapter
- Taking notes from a textbook
- Cleaning up your room
- Doing laundry
- Fighting less with a parent or sibling

	ACTIVITIES I PROCRASTINATE
1	
2	
3	

Gather Materials

Some helpful materials are:

- Your favorite color pencils, markers, or gel pens (not necessary, but definitely playful)
- Blank paper or the template of the wheel below
- Some calming or upbeat background music (again, not necessary, but very playful)

Draw a Wheel

Use the template on the next page or draw your own. Add an activity in the center that would make your life work better if it were easier to get started on it without procrastinating.

Fill the Spokes with Prototypes

Break up the activity into actions that take five minutes or less to complete. Check out the example above. If you only had five minutes to do something related to this activity, what would it be?

Shrink it down to one of the smallest possible steps, so it's a little easier to handle. You're not trying to do the whole thing here. Just do one little bit. Then, you can do the next little bit after. An object in motion stays in motion. Well, that's physics, but in our circumstance, it is definitely a lot easier to keep going once you get through that first step.

"It's that first step — getting out the door — that's the toughest. If you can do that, you've already won." (Mary J. Blige n.d.)

My Sun-beaming Wheel

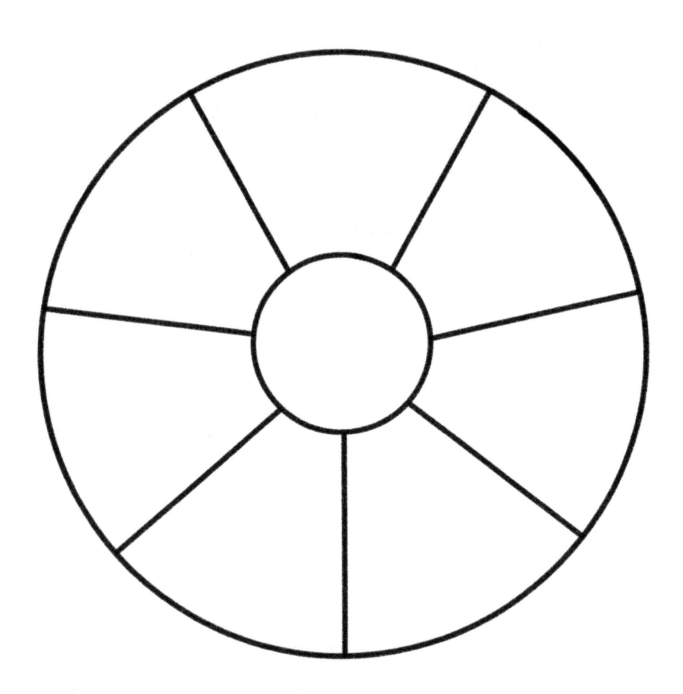

Exercise 2: Big Celebrations for Small Wins

Playing with mini-sized things is just plain ol' fun. This is good news because in life, the small things end up being the big things. Our small, everyday actions really matter. So, in this exercise, we are going to act like it and get playful about how we celebrate our tiny victories. Getting playful makes it more likely that you will repeat the effective behaviors. The celebration increases the natural feel-good chemicals in our nervous system including *dopamine, serotonin, oxytocin, and endorphins*. Our brain uses those as signals to remember to do more of the activity that produced the chemicals.

I'm going to be honest. Most people want to skip this exercise because it seems so "after the fact," but it's where the magic happens. Throughout your day, find ways to congratulate yourself like you just won a major award for all the small, everyday things that are aligned with your goals or values.

Methods

1. Do one small thing that's aligned with one of your goals.
2. Come up with your mini-celebration routine.
3. Remember to celebrate throughout the day with a remember-to-remember cue.
4. Linger and savor it.

Do One Small, Good Thing That's Aligned with One of Your Goals

This one is straightforward. Do just one small thing. Here's a list to get your mind going about what that could be:

- Hold the door open for someone
- Volunteer to help with something small in the classroom like putting chairs up or venturing to answer a question that's getting met with awkward silence
- Start a long-term assignment the day it's assigned, just for 10 minutes to get the ball rolling
- Spend 10 minutes during homework time rereading class notes, adding pictures, symbols, and questions, as well as highlighting key terms
- Make five flashcards for a test that isn't happening for another week or so
- Stop, breathe, and tell yourself something kind when you catch yourself in negative self-talk
- Get to class a couple minutes before it starts to check out what's on the board, smile at the teacher, and get yourself settled before it begins
- Organize your things for the next day and putting them by the door before you go to bed
- Notice yourself going for your phone, and taking a moment to ask yourself the three Ws from Catherine Price's *How to Break Up with your Phone*: "What for? Why now? What else?" If you can't come up with good answers, do some stretching or go talk to someone who's around in person instead.
- Take three mindful breaths. Slowly breathe in, filling up your belly. Relax your body on the out breath. Notice how it feels as the breath moves in and out of your body.

What's one small thing you plan on doing that you can celebrate? Create a mental picture in your head of the time, place, sights, and sounds around you as you do that thing.

My one small, good thing will be...	

Come Up with Your Mini-Celebration Routine

When was the last time you experienced something great? It could be something you put in a lot of effort to accomplish or something that just popped up out of the blue to your great delight and surprise.

What do you do when you win a match, nail a performance, dominate in a video game, or get permission to do something you've been wanting to do for a while? What sounds or exclamations do you make? What gestures do you make with your body? What does your face do? How do you feel inside, and where do you feel it most?

For me, it's a "yay!" and a vigorous clap that my kids tell me is supernaturally and embarrassingly loud. I feel excitement in my chest, kind of like someone flipped on a power switch and it filled with light.

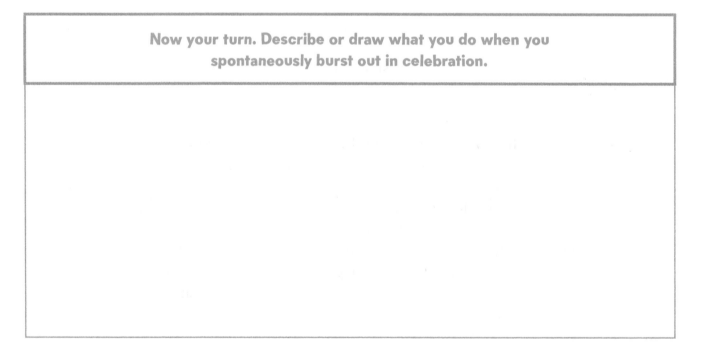

Now your turn. Describe or draw what you do when you
spontaneously burst out in celebration.

That's what we're going for here, but I realize you might be in the middle of a quiet classroom. Let's come up with a version that dials down the physical loudness (if needed), but still manages to amplify that internal feeling of *yes!*

What's your mini celebration for your one small thing? Describe or draw it below:

Guess what? You just did one small, good thing aligned with your goals, just by thinking about this. So, do it now! Celebrate. Really, practice your mini celebration right now!

Remember-to-Remember Cue

This practice is new. It won't seem urgent, which means you're likely to forget to do it. To remember, you're going to pick a cue that occurs throughout your day to remind you of it. Here are some examples of remember-to-remember cues you can attach to this new thing you want to try:

- Wear a string or new band around your wrist
- The passing bells at school
- Phone bleeps and blorps — your own or others
- When you notice a certain color
- If you're me right now, every time you hear a leaf blower (those things are always going off in my neighborhood)

What will be your remember-to-remember cue?

Linger and Savor

So, you've done the good thing. The cue has kept your celebration top of mind and you actually do it. Don't rush on yet. The act of savoring is psychologically proven to get good feelings to stick. So we not only get the happiness benefits for longer, but our brain also starts encoding the action related to that good feeling. That gets us to start doing it more automatically in the future. Here are a few tips to practice savoring:

- Notice the details your senses are picking up on a little more than you normally would — sights, sounds, tastes, physical sensations, and smells.
- Express gratitude. Even just quietly in your mind for a moment. Say, "Thank you." I even like to say, "Ooh, thanks! More of this, please!"

Exercise 3: Develop a Curiosity Habit

It's hard to pay attention to something for long if we're not a little curious about it first. Back when we were expert players as kids, we were curious all the time. We had the wiring for natural curiosity back in the incessant "why" phase of our childhood development. Why are stop signs shaped like that? How did swear words become so different from other words? Why did people choose to wear such uncomfortable clothes in Victorian England?

Okay. I'll admit those just came from my old adult brain, but only because I've rewired it to get very quickly into a playful, curious mode when I want to. And I want you to start retraining your brain to remember how to be curious about things, too.

Method

1. Identify and pursue natural interests.
2. Play the "how is this like that?" game.
3. Preview with curiosity.

Identify and Pursue Natural Interests

It sounds obvious, but the older we get, the more "stuff" we feel is a more important use of our time and focus. To be a more curious person, we have to practice what it's like to engage our curiosity muscle. It's a lot easier to do when it's a topic or activity you're naturally curious about. Maybe you already know what those interest are. But if you don't, it's okay. Here are some questions and examples to get your mind turning about it:

- What did you used to love to do when you were younger?
- If you still had to go to school, but you got to choose what you learned about, what subjects or topics would you pick?
- Who is one of the most interesting people you know in real life, history, or someone famous? What are their interests?
- What are some issues in the world that just really irk you and that you wish were better?
- If you had all the time in the world to give it a try, what is the weirdest, most unexpected topic or activity that interests you?

Name one to three interests in the table below.

MY INTERESTS	
1	
2	
3	

That's really all you need to identify for now. If you want to take it up a notch, commit to spending 15 minutes a week learning or practicing one of those topics.

Play the "How Is This Like That?" Game

Pick something you are learning, like the quadratic formula, and then see how many connections you can make between that and something that you enjoy and know a lot about. If it's a little hard to find the similarities, that's good. It means your neural networks are stretching, and your memory for the new thing you need to learn is getting stronger.

How is this like that?

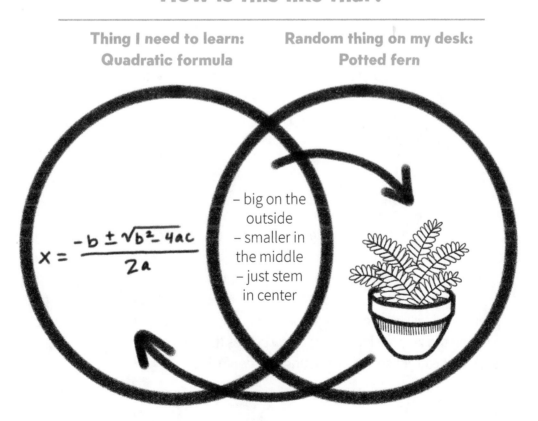

Thing I need to learn:
Quadratic formula

Random thing on my desk:
Potted fern

$$x = \frac{-b \pm \sqrt{b^2 - 4ac}}{2a}$$

– big on the outside
– smaller in the middle
– just stem in center

How is this like that?

Thing I need to learn: **Random thing on my desk:**

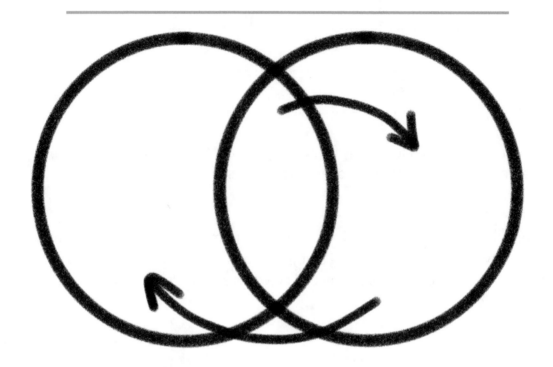

Preview with Curiosity

Previewing means seeing something before it becomes generally known or available. When previewing with curiosity, it's like a fun sneak peek that's also really good for learning and processing information.

Here are some ways to practice previewing with curiosity:

- Before the teacher starts the class, check for cues in the room on the topic for the day. Think of a question or opinion you have about it already.
- Print out teacher-provided slides or notes before the class. Mark them up by hand with what you already know or think you might know about it in the margins. When you go over it in class, take notes that either confirm or correct what you thought.
- Find some good old-fashioned chapter guide questions online to go along with that book you're reading in English. Read them before you read the chapter. Googling "book title + teacher guide" will give me straightforward questions that are much more practical and useful than those sprawling online study guides (the ones with all their links and bells and whistles that can get sort of distracting and confusing).

- Look up a quick video or even a deeper-dive documentary about the unit or topic you're about to study. With pictures and a whole soundtrack, all that new information will stick to what's already in your head.
- If you have a textbook, scan over the pictures and graphics and take guesses about what those are all about before learning that section in class.

Whichever preview method you choose or make your own, be sure to do it with a spirit of curiosity — more of an "I wonder" than "I have to know."

Bonus Method: Alien Questioning

When you're really at a loss, try asking questions like an alien who has never been to Earth. Take one or two minutes to brainstorm before class or doing schoolwork. The goal is to beat boredom and wake up your curiosity and motivation.

Alien Questions:

- Who came up with algebra and why?
- Why do some cultures read right to left, but others read left to right?
- Why did this author come up with the idea to write this book?
- Why does my teacher think it's important for me to know this?
- Why are some numbers curvy and some are angular?

EXAMPLE		YOUR TURN	
Turning irrational numbers into fractions		Topic:	
1	Who came up with the idea of fractions and what did it help them do?	1	
2	When did people start using decimals and why?	2	
3	I wonder if anyone has made art out of irrational numbers. What that would look like?	3	

Be Unavailable for Boredom

My student Mike let his Chinese homework pile up. He could get 90 percents on the tests without doing homework because he understood it already. The repetitive practice of stuff he had already mastered was a task he dreaded. The problem was that homework counted for 40 percent of his grade, so even with a 90 percent test average, his grade was in the 60s. He was in danger of having to repeat a class he already understood really well. When he started homework, Mike assumed the position of dread and boredom. You know the one — shoulders hunched, head hung low resting on his arm, and his pencil slowly dragging across the paper while his eyes drooped. One worksheet down, three more to go at 11 pm. His memory of the experience confirmed how terrible it was, making it easy for him to block out that item on his to-do list when it came up again.

We need to talk about boredom for a minute. One of the biggest obstacles to my students' happiness is boredom. Most don't know this, but they are often afraid of being bored. Like Mike, the cave person part of their brain will pull out all the stops to avoid boredom, because it believes that if they get bored, they might become less alert and more likely to get pounced on by a cheetah. That very old, prehistoric part of your brain is straight up uncomfortable with boredom. Fear will always lead to procrastination, but joy and play will motivate.

Fear of Being Weird

Speaking of fear, a fear of being weird is another common block to playfulness. Have you ever watched young kids on a playground? They get weird. They invent outlandish games with incomprehensible rules, act like creatures only they can see in their heads, say nonsense words, yell and scream and laugh and mumble to themselves. It's a trip. Anyhow, I'm not suggesting that we go about acting like that everywhere. I do think we start to lose that wild abandon for play as we get older and have more fears about being judged by others or not fitting in. Those things that make us a little weird are also what we can do to make things more fun.

Now that I'm well into my 40s, most days my idea of fun is getting to hang out in a comfortable chair, so I'm probably not going to be very good at coming up with what would make things more fun for you. In my family, after failing miserably to impress my kids with things I thought were spectacular, I ended up coming up with a motto for vacations: everyone is responsible for their own fun.

Making things fun in your own weird way is how you make things meaningful. You're taking something that's just sitting there flat on paper, in a book, or on a recording and creating a brand-new experience out of it. I find it inspiring that we all have the potential to take information or assignments that have been there for a long, long, long time and make something totally new from them based on our own personal weird stamp.

Teachers, bless our hearts, will try to make things fun. We sometimes succeed and a lot of times hilariously, spectacularly fail.

So, you're going to take the wheel on this one, rather than relying on us old people to make things more fun and meaningful for you. We won't be as good at it as you are. And while you're at it, remember — the weirder the better.

> **Sidebar: Because I can't help myself, here's a little more etymology for you (again, this is why you don't want to rely on teachers like me to make things fun for you — learning etymology is another way I have fun).**
>
> **The ancestor of the word "weird" is wyrd, which comes from Old English meaning to preordain a fate or destiny. So basically if you were wyrd, you were super wise and gifted. There's another reason to make things a little weird and be unavailable for boredom.**

Being playful in our own weird way is about joy and happiness. While we're on the topic of happiness, here's a thought I want you to put in your head. Observe how it makes you feel:

> **You get to relax now.**
>
> **You get to feel good now.**
>
> **You don't have to wait.**

If that makes you feel more spacious, open, or good, then keep thinking it. Write it down where you can see it and see what little actions it inspires you to take.

However, if you're like most of us, it might bring up a whole lot of "but resistance."

Giving Up "But Resistance"

No, this is not a glutes exercise. "But resistance" is another one of those fear-based thoughts that was programmed into you by your culture and upbringing to try to keep you in line. It gets in the way of playing. "But resistance" might sound something like this:

- But, if I relax now, then I won't get anything done.
- But, if we all just walk around doing what makes us feel good, then we'll all be running around addicted to drugs, without our clothes on, stealing whatever we want from each other.
- But, if I did what I really wanted, then I'd just blow off all my classes and homework and fail out of school. Then my parents will send me to some sort of scared straight program where they make me walk for miles in the woods before 5 am and wash floors in between grueling, mind-numbing classes where the teachers yell at you to shape up or ship out.

Oh, was that last one just me because of my mom's threat to send me to a convent every time I slipped up?

These thoughts aren't always bad, because they do sometimes signal something we need to acknowledge. Taking drugs, stealing, and running around naked is not where we want to end up eventually. The drugs will ruin your essential organs and relationships, the stealing will hurt other people, and the nakedness, well? I guess you'll risk frostbite and social ostracization.

But you see, those self-destructive behaviors aren't about feeling good and relaxing. Those are things people sometimes do when they don't believe in their ability to feel good and relaxed in the present moment (or have fair and equitable access to it). Escaping or numbing out from the present reality seems like a better option. The same goes for the fear that you can either blow off all your homework and classes and fail out of school or feel good, relaxed, and playful. Deep down, you know that blowing off all your responsibilities will hurt your life more than it will help it. It won't feel all that good for long. It's not your craving for more joy and peace that causes you to procrastinate. It's your fear that you won't have enough of it. I see so many students, and I've been one of them, too, who have a hard time getting started because they fear that schoolwork will take up all their available time. What if the prospect of doing schoolwork wasn't laden with so much fear of getting it wrong, boredom, and frustration? What if you had the power to make it feel a little more playful and less stressful? I believe play is an excellent cure for procrastination.

If you're like most humans, you want to create a good life for yourself, so letting yourself get a little silly with the work when those fear-based feelings start to surface won't cause too much damage. You won't go too far with it and tank your grades if you allow yourself a little fun with it.

Go ahead and let your fears bring up some potential dangers for your consideration. You can put some safeguards around what you are afraid of if there's some reason for them, but don't let your fear of boredom be the one in control around here. Approaching these tasks with a more playful perspective could take the sting of fear out of them.

Exercise 1: Gamify the Boring Stuff

To be clear, I am not a gamer in the computer or console sense of the word. I have a tendency to shut computers down by looking in their direction. Seriously, now when my husband is updating or downloading something on his computer, he'll ask me to go into another room. There are all sorts of apps that help people gamify their habits, goals, and study efforts. For our purposes here, when I talk about gamifying something, I think about that playground I mentioned earlier where the kids feel free to let their weird out. When schoolwork or other responsibilities feel heavy, try applying a gaming mindset to it. A gaming mindset says:

- Just try it. See if it's any fun.
- Mistakes are to be expected. Just try again. No biggie.
- This will have a definite beginning and end.
- Ooh. I want to try to get better at this, just because it's fun to feel like I'm getting better at something.

Methods

1. Create your playground.
2. Use a "play again" mindset.
3. Add points!
4. Get some teammates.
5. Give it a beginning and ending.

Create Your Playground

A playground is a place where you feel relaxed. It has structures around it, so that it's safe and inspires ideas for play. Let's apply this to create a homework playground.

What's a simple and easy thing that helps you feel relaxed? Here are some examples:

- Soothing music
- A pet nearby
- Bustling background noise
- A nice window to look out of

What's something relaxing I can add to my homework playground?	

What are some materials that would inspire a little more "play" for your homework playground? Here are some examples:

- A whiteboard with colorful markers
- Colored pencils or pens
- A stability ball chair to sit and bounce
- Playdough (seriously, I've seen students use playdough to make models of things they needed to learn)
- A kitchen timer
- A standing desk

My homework playground structures:	

Use a "Play Again" Mindset

When you lose at Pac-Man, (remember I told you I'm really not a gamer, so that's my reference point) the screen doesn't flash and say, "That's it for you, loser! You better never show your face around here again." No, it says some version of: "Play again!" When you're playing a game, yes, you might want to win, but it's not like you put all this pressure on yourself that depends on winning. One outcome doesn't make you a good or bad person, or a success or failure in all of life. That's because you don't attach everything about your whole identity and future to a game.

Here's a trick to help you apply that same attitude to schoolwork:

Think of a plan B. Set your goal for a habit, test, or project, but then ask yourself these questions and imagine the answers in your head. Then, write those down below.

If this doesn't go the way I want, how can I react or respond so I can still stay on track for my goals?

What are some reasons why I can still succeed if this doesn't go well?

Add Points

Games motivate us to become experts, not just because they are inherently fun, but also because they give us points. Getting points is fun and satisfying. My favorite way to add points to something is with stickers. Here's how:

- Go get a huge pack of whichever ones you find delightful.
- Use them to reward yourself for small tasks or habits completed.
- For every 20 minutes of focused study time, put a sticker on note card or your hand (or forehead, even) and see how many you can accumulate.

- Write down the habit you're trying, and put a note card in where the habit should take place. Every time you do it, add a sticker.
- Compete with a friend or family member and compare sticker amounts.

> **What's something challenging, difficult, or hard to change that you'd like to make a habit?**

> **Why is this important to you?**

> **How can you give yourself points for following through on it? What small step will you take that will be point-worthy?**

Give It a Beginning and End

When we start a game, we know it won't go on forever. It has a definite beginning and end. Do the same with your schoolwork. Rather than thinking about getting your schoolwork done in terms of task completion, think about it in time segments. When there's an assignment to do, estimate a reasonable amount of time to spend on it by asking yourself these questions before you get started:

- How long do I think this should take?
- Is it best for me to do this all in one go, or should I break it up in chunks?
- What's the best chunk for me to do now, and how long would that take?

Then set a timer and go!

> **For a longer list student-inspired ways to gamify school tasks, check out the book bonuses: h2c.ai/hgw**

Put It All Together

Imagine a friend comes to you complaining about how they have to do a task below, but it makes them want to stick a pencil through their eye because it's so boring. (Don't do this. I have been in this business so long, I knew a student who really did poke their eye with a pencil by accident, and it was not pretty. He recovered, but I'm not sure I did). Give them some ways to gamify the activities below. Feel free to steal or modify any of the ideas above.

ACTIVITY	GAMIFY IT
Taking notes in class	
Studying for a test	
Writing an essay	

Exercise 2: Introduce Some Novelty

Novelty means something that feels new and fresh. When my kids were little, I realized that I didn't need to keep buying them new toys when they got bored with their old ones. I just had to make their old ones seem new again by hiding some away for a week and then switching them out with the others. This doesn't mean you should hide your homework away for a week and then bring it back out for the fun of it. That won't work. But the concept of novelty will. Your brain loves shiny new objects that capture its attention and interest. Here are three key places to introduce novelty in order to avoid boredom.

Methods

1. New tools
2. New environment
3. New routine

Your Tools

You'd be surprised how much more playful and interesting homework can be when you bring new supplies into the mix. Having a couple of fresh new tools around you can inspire you to get more creative and playful with your work. Below are some of my favorites.

- Note cards in different colors
- A whiteboard and markers
- Post-it notes or index cards in different colors
- A colorful keyboard cover
- Colored pens or pencils
- A large desk-sized paper pad

Your Environment

- Stick around in the library at school or go to a coffee shop.
- Move from room to room every 30 minutes or when you switch subjects.
- Bring something cozy or pleasant like a blanket, favorite photo, or plant into the place where you do your homework.
- Post inspiring quotes, your goals, or photos of people who inspire you around your workspace.

Your Routine

Change up the order you usually do things. If you usually start with the hardest, start with the easiest, or vice versa. Or try going back and forth.

- If you usually do work after a snack and some screen time, try doing one thing first and then grabbing a snack.
- If you tend to save your reading for nighttime, move it up to during the day.
- Try doing some homework before school or during breaks and lunch.
- If you usually do work silently, try talking out loud while you solve problems or read. If you usually type out your responses to homework questions, try using the voice to text option instead.

What's one thing you can add or change to add some novelty to your schoolwork?	

And remember, even the new stuff will get old, so don't be afraid to change it up every week if you need!

Exercise 3: Fake It, Until You Make It

If you're finding it hard to drum up the fun, you can also try to fake it till you make it. I used to do this when I was in high school. I did my homework as if I was an actor in a movie about a super-smart, expert historian, mathematician, or chemist. I never told anyone because I thought I was just a weirdo, but I was a weirdo who was managing to get through boring homework with less distractions. Later I read the verifiable strategy researched by psychologists in Amy Cuddy's book *Presence*. One of my favorite points from Cuddy is that it's not so much faking it till you make it, but instead faking it until you become it. Your movement, speech, and posture give your brain signals about how to feel, which informs who we become. Simply experimenting with this strategy in little ways will benefit you with motivation and happiness.

Methods

1. Define how you want to be as a person.
2. Think of a model person who is like that.
3. Identify a current challenge you wish you could handle better.
4. Imagine how your model would handle it, and decide on one small thing you can try.

Think about How You Want to Be as a Person

List those words below. You can find a list of "being" words in the book bonuses for inspiration.

HOW I WANT TO BE

Think of a Model Person Who Is Like That

This person can be real or fictional. They can be someone in your life right now or someone you don't know personally, but know about. It's okay if that person is totally different from you. They are just a model.

Identify a Current Challenge You Wish You Could Handle Better

Try to think about a challenge that's somewhat in your control but would make your life run better if you could handle it in a better way. For example, you might not be able to change the fact that your social studies teacher talks way too fast for you to understand. You can still find a way to get the information you need, in the way you need it to be prepared for the test. Don't worry about how you'll handle it yet. Just think of a situation that you wish you could make better.

What's a current situation that challenges you or bums you out that you wish you could handle better?

Imagine How Your Model Would Handle It

> Draw a scene (stick figures are fine) where your model is in that situation
> and handling it like a pro. Label their facial expressions, actions, body language,
> and posture. Add a thought bubble that includes what they're thinking during
> the situation.

Now pick just one small thing from the picture above that you can see yourself doing.

> One area in my life that I can experiment with fake it till you make it is:

User Warning:
One little caveat about the "fake it till you make it"
method. Please don't try to fake it until you make it
when it comes to your emotions. If you're feeling sad
or frustrated, pretending like you aren't having those
feelings will only make them come back even stronger.

Section 2 Reflection

What are the main ideas or points that seem important to you?	Why is something you read about particularly important or relevant to you?
When might you use something you learned?	**Who could you reach out to for help? Can you think of anyone you could help with something you learned?**

P.S. Taking five minutes to fill out a what, who, when, why chart at the end of any section you've read for school is a quick way to make what you read stick. You can always substitute a different question to fit the reading, such as: What were the main points? Who were the most important people involved? When did the important things take place? Why does it matter?

Our next section is going to give you some suggestions for feeling emotions without getting overwhelmed or letting them derail you from your goals. On top of helping you deal with emotions, it will also give you more inspiration for making things less boring.

GET PLAYFUL KEY TAKEAWAYS	
Make small prototypes of big tasks. The small things are the big things.	
1	Celebrate your small wins. Taking a moment to feel how great it is to act toward your goals will signal your brain to motivate you to do it again.
2	Develop a curiosity habit. Ask questions before learning something to make it more interesting and easier to remember.
3	Use a gaming mindset. Replace the heaviness of needing to do things you aren't naturally interested in by making a game out of it. Make a game you can play again if you didn't get it right the first time.
4	Embrace novelty. We pay more attention to shiny new objects. Keep your goal consistent, and feel free to occasionally change things up to help your attention and motivation.
5	Fake it till you make it with small, inspired actions, but not emotions. Take a break from the part of yourself that gets bored and disheartened by schoolwork, and pretend to be someone who's really great at it. You might discover a different part of yourself that already is.

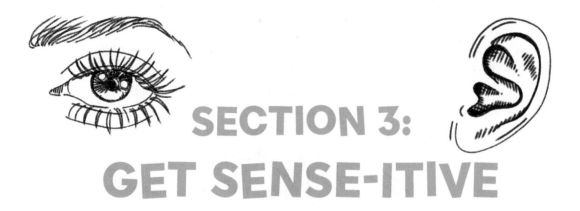

SECTION 3:
GET SENSE-ITIVE

- When you think of someone who is sensitive, what picture comes to mind?
- Do you notice anything weird about the way I spelled sense-itive? Want to take a guess on why I spelled it that way?

IN THIS SECTION, YOU'LL LEARN ABOUT:	
1	**How to use the strong emotions you've got going on for good**
	The RAIN process to help you get through those low moments in life with more happiness and resilience
	Mental contrasting so you can be realistically optimistic
	Increase your overall happiness and resilience by soaking up the good with the HEAL process
2	**How to use your physical senses to improve motivation, focus, and memory when you study, do homework, and take tests**
	Study strategies that use your senses
	Rituals for more focus and motivation when you do homework and take tests
	Using story to remember important information

Get Sense-itive Pep Talk

I was a teenager in the height of the grunge period in the 90s, so when I hear the word sensitive, I see lots of angsty, emo-type artists.

Now there are a lot of moody artists creating meaningful, valuable work out there, so brood-on if you want to. But, when it comes to creating happy grades, I'm talking about sensitive with the emphasis on the "sense" part of the word. Scientists know that the more senses we use in the learning process, the stronger the neural pathways.

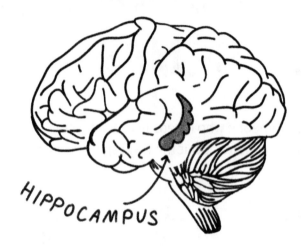

HIPPOCAMPUS

You see that thing deep in the center of our brain? It's called the hippocampus. I know it looks tiny, but it's important. One critical job it has is to put memories in our brain for the long term, so they can be useful to us later. Now read this quote. I warn you, it's super brain scientist-y, so just go with it for a second and then I'll explain:

> "Until recently, the brain was thought to have separate learning systems, but the findings suggest the hippocampal memory system and striatal reinforcement learning system are interrelated" (Science Daily 2019).

Huh? Not to worry, I've got you. It means that the way we learn is a whole nervous system experience. It involves our whole bodies, informed by how we feel, smell, touch, taste, hear, and touch. It depends on all our senses, not just in the thinking part of our brain.

The best way to learn something is to make a whole-body experience of it — something you can feel physically and emotionally. Use as many senses as you can get into the mix, rather than just thinking super hard about it. The bad news is this requires a little more proactive effort on your part to make it happen — it's a little more active than just going over it. The good news is it makes your school life more creative and interesting. There are some simple ways to do it that we're going to get into in this section.

The way your brain develops at this phase of your life, how you feel, and your sense of belonging with others takes up a lot of your focus. Sometimes I wish there was a whole class period per day in high school and college dedicated to teachers and students simply naming all the little annoying and disappointing mistakes and circumstances that happened that day that didn't turn out the way they planned it. Then, maybe we wouldn't all be walking around thinking that we're the weird ones who don't belong because we're somehow not as bright, competent, or normal as everyone else.

We could sit around for 45 minutes or so and listen to each other say things like, "I actually studied for that quiz, but misread a question and got a whole 20 points off since there were only five questions." Or, "I walked around all day with a black bean stuck between my teeth and taught four classes that way, and nobody told me." And we'd chuckle a little, give each other pats on the back, and exclaim, "Same!"

We wouldn't give each other unsolicited advice or judge each other. We'd just help each other feel lighter about life. We'd see that this stuff happens to the best of us. We can try to do better with more love and compassion for ourselves because we see how lovely, funny, and beautiful others are when they share their flawed, imperfect lives. Can you see why I wasn't the best at being a traditional teacher? That's my idea of an awesome use of class time.

If you don't have a class like that, there are proven strategies that teach you how to bring that sense of comfort, belonging, and resilience to yourself when you need it.

Tap into Your Emotions

Before we get into your physical senses, we're going to tap into another super powerful sense. Beyond the realm of hearing, sight, touch, taste, and smell, we have another sense that is strongly tied to learning and memory.

No, I'm not talking about psychic abilities, but if you are gifted in that way, then do what works!

The non-physical sense I'm talking about is your emotions. Emotional memory is a super strength we humans have. We store emotional memories deep in a prehistoric part of our brain called the *amygdala*. It's great because it protects us from physical and emotional trauma without us even having to think about it. It likes to make our memories with strong emotional senses super resistant to forgetting. If we have an experience that makes us feel insecure, threatened, rejected, or another difficult emotion, the amygdala will make sure you avoid that kind of scenario. If you have an experience that's charged with a lot of laughter, love, excitement, or other happiness-infused emotions, it will remember that too, so you can repeat it.

Unfortunately, the amygdala has a proclivity to hold on to the negative things way more than the positive. Your amygdala doesn't care about how you do on tests or in school. It just wants you to stay safe and alive. Since you care how you do in school, you can train it to work for you for that purpose.

Negative Emotions

First let's address negative emotions. In addition to keeping you safe and away from threats, which is a good thing, your amygdala might also read simple, even potentially good things as signals to do whatever it takes to get out of the situation. Again, that can sometimes be a good and protective thing your body does, so we don't want to ignore the amygdala's warning system altogether. However, it hasn't evolved yet in our modern times to know the difference between a real threat and an uncomfortable task that's just sort of boring or hard, even if it can help us grow and achieve a goal. Some potentially good things it might want you to avoid, that you encounter all the time as a student, include but are not limited to:

- Being bored
- A weird look on someone's face (that could be them feeling awkward, but your amygdala might read it as they are plotting something against you)
- When the room gets too noisy or too quiet for your personal comfort level
- A comment on your work to watch out for careless errors
- Taking tests and quizzes
- A bunch of critical corrections all over a draft you handed in that your teacher wants you to rewrite
- Going to a social event

If you pay close attention, you can notice what the amygdala alarm feels like in your body before you even get a conscious signal in your brain to do something about it. For me, I either feel like there's a small but hot stone in the center of my belly or a twist tie sealing off a space at the base of my throat so that air can only get in around the sides.

My amygdala is super dramatic, I know, so I really need to help myself out and identify what that feeling is really signaling — when I should run for the hills because someone is about to attack me, versus when I'm just trying to avoid feeling awkward by talking to the people in the car shop about getting my tires rotated. Enough about me, though, let's try some ways to get that emotional center of your brain to work for you.

Taking Advantage of Positive Emotions

It's not like we never have any positive emotions. However, our brains are programmed with a negativity bias, so it can sure feel like that sometimes. A negativity bias means our brain holds on to negative memories way more than positive ones. Remember that the amygdala is just trying to keep us safe. It's way more focused on getting us to avoid actions and circumstances that might make us feel bad than the actions or situations that could make us feel happy, accomplished, and successful. Much of the research shows that our brains will hang on to the negative stuff from our day. We remember the teacher who gave you the evil eye in class, the question you lost points on because you didn't read it correctly, and the two minutes you walked around after lunch with food stuck in your teeth before you realized it in the bathroom mirror. The positive experiences from the day — the teacher who said you had a good point when you spoke up in class, the majority of questions on the quiz you handled correctly, or the way it felt good to laugh with friends at lunch — will pretty much get filtered out of our brain's memory system like they never happened.

This means we have to try extra hard to encode the positive experiences, so our brains hang on to those memories, too. The actions and experiences that lead us to feelings of happiness and success can be quite instructive. Those positive memories can help us remember what worked last time, so we do it again and don't feel so down and out when things get hard. This is called resilience, and it's a vital quality to cultivate for living a happy and successful life. Academic resilience means sustaining high levels of motivation and persistence towards a goal even when facing conditions or circumstances that could threaten your ability to do well (Alva, 1991). That could come in pretty handy when you're faced with a teacher who just doesn't teach in a way that helps you make sense of things or when stressful events happen in your family or social life. The good news is that developing resilience doesn't just have to come from toughing out difficult circumstances. That helps, but only if you recognize and absorb your positive strengths and resources that got you through. You can build resilience through positive experiences as well (Fredrickson, 2001).

Exercise 1: RAIN

Get a sense of what your amygdala alarm feels like. Think about the last time you faced a situation that you wanted to avoid. What did that feel like in your body? Where in your body did you feel it the most?

If you could give it some physical qualities (sharp, soft, round, rough, pointy, heavy), what does it feel like? Sometimes giving it physical qualities can help you feel more in control of it, so it doesn't take over your whole nervous system and derail you for too long. Once you have a good sense of when your amygdala alarm is starting up, you can use RAIN to bring yourself back into a calm state.

"All these responses reflect our natural resistance to feeling uncomfortable and unsafe: thoughts swarm in our head, we leave our body, we judge what is happening" (Brach 2011).

Method

Now that you're developing a good sense of how to detect your negative emotions, you're ready to use a process called RAIN to deal with it. This can be done either in your head or in writing. You can use the exercises below to practice. Then apply this process any moment in the future when you detect a negative emotion getting in your way of moving toward your goals.

1. Recognize.
2. Allow.
3. Investigate.
4. Nurture.

R - Recognize

Think of the last time your emotions got the better of you. Maybe it was when you were taking a test and your nerves got in the way of what you were able to remember the night before when studying. Or, maybe it was when you had some homework to do but were dreading the boredom or frustration of it, so you put it off for too long. Apply these questions to that situation as if you were in the moment.

- What is happening inside you right now? Try to describe what it feels like.
- Where are you feeling it?
- Can you give it a color or compare it to a shape or object?

A - Allow

Tell yourself to let it be there for now. Don't try to rush it off or push it away. You won't want to do this, because it feels uncomfortable at first. You'll find that by taking a few deep breaths and letting it just be the way it is, it takes the fight out of you. You'll feel like it gets a little softer and easier to feel.

If you took those first two steps, you are probably already feeling better. Congratulations on how resilient you're becoming. These next two steps supersize the effects of this tool. They help you deal when the same feeling comes back again with even more strength and resilience.

I - Investigate

Ask yourself or ask the feeling as if it was a small, anxious child or animal of your choice. In other words, be as gentle and kind as you can.

- What thoughts are you having right now that are making you feel bad?
- How would you feel without that thought?
- What do you need in order to feel better?

N - Nurture

Now, give that little wounded thought-animal some big-time love and kindness. You can send yourself loving, warm feelings by imagining a time you felt really good, loved, safe, and happy. Take a few moments remembering it and feeling it as if you were there.

> **You can also nurture yourself by doing a two-minute battery recharge. A recharge can be getting a hug, listening to a guided meditation, looking at some pictures that make you happy, getting outside to breathe some fresh air and look up at the sky and trees, or giving a pet a good cuddle.**

One of the strongest research-based ways to nurture yourself is with kind self-talk. This is when you talk to yourself like you would talk to someone you really love. It works best when you do it in third person: "Tricia, you are doing your best and even though this rewrite is taking a long time, it's going to be worth it!" (Sorry, I needed to do a little nurturing of myself just now). Name three ideas below you can use to nurture yourself.

HOW I CAN NURTURE MYSELF	
1	
2	
3	

Exercise 2: Mental Contrasting

Chances are you've heard of the importance of a *growth mindset*. It's a term used a lot now in school. Carol Dweck, the psychologist who led the research studies and wrote the book about it, had to come out of retirement to tell us that we had overgeneralized the whole thing and were kind of getting it wrong. "Growth mindset" turned into just another way to say "think positive" in order to achieve hard things. It was sort of like those "hang in there" cat posters in my high school counselor's office that are now ironic GIFs to send a friend when they're having a hard time. It's a way to paste a bumper sticker over your confusion and frustration about the aspects of school you find most challenging. It just doesn't work and can even sometimes make it even harder to get motivated and stick with positive behaviors for happiness and success. A better approach to achieving big dreams and goals is called *mental contrasting*.

> "We would be wrong to jettison our dreams, just as we are wrong to blindly assume that simply dreaming something can make it so" (Oettingen 2014).

Method

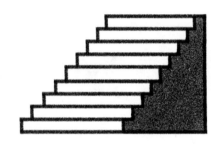

1. Identify your dream, wish, or goal.
2. Identify the obstacles.
3. Strategize the small steps.
4. Make an if/then plan.

Identify Your Dream, Wish, or Goal

Think of a personal goal. It can be a big, long-term dream, a smaller goal you have for yourself just for the week, or somewhere in the middle. Think of something you'd like to achieve that would make your life work a little better or make you feel happier about how things are going. It should be a little bit of a stretch, but something you think is doable. Give yourself permission to be positive here. Visualize yourself being happy and satisfied with the result that's made a positive difference.

My goal, wish, or dream is:

Apply positive thinking liberally here!

Identify the Obstacles

At this point, if you're like most of us, this might cause a few uncomfortable things to happen. You might receive a bunch of thoughts about why that goal, wish, or dream is impossible, silly, or at the very least, highly unlikely because of how you are or have been in the past. You might start thinking about all the things besides yourself that could get in your way. You might get a general feeling of anxiety or stress about it, which is a signal that these thoughts are coming, but they aren't clear to you yet. All these things are your predicted obstacles. As uncomfortable as they are to notice, they're helpful to identify.

What are the obstacles I think could get in my way to doing, being, or having my goal, wish, or dream?	

One important note here — make sure that the obstacles you identify are things you have some amount of control over. Yes, a natural disaster or your dog throwing up on your project could get in your way, but things we can't control cause worry, and we're going for inspired, powerful action here.

Strategize the Small Steps

Think about the small steps you could take to get around, over, or through that obstacle. What have you done in the past that has worked in that situation? What have you heard about as a strategy? Keep that strategy small and practical. If you're stuck here, go ask for advice from someone you trust. This is usually my favorite part of sessions with students. It's fun and powerful to brainstorm ideas together, so I highly recommend bringing in someone else. If you get stuck here, you can also try coming up with the most ridiculous strategies first. Those can open up your creative mind. You might be surprised what you come up with that could actually work.

Small steps around, through, or over that obstacle:	

Make an If/Then Plan

If/then planning is a powerful strategy for sticking with a new positive habit. It's backed up by lots of psychological research. My favorite thing is it's super simple. I love how it takes the obstacle you predicted and turns it into a positive opportunity to try out a strategy.

IF (MY OBSTACLE HAPPENS),	THEN I WILL (SMALL STRATEGY).
If. . .	then I will. . .
,	.

It helps if you mentally rehearse that if/then plan by visualizing the scenario and seeing yourself implementing the strategy. Writing your if/then plan on a Post-it and sticking that somewhere you'll see it often is also helpful.

Exercise 3: HEAL

Here's a feel-good twist on mental contrasting developed by Rick Hanson, psychologist, author, and senior fellow at the Greater Good Science Center at Berkeley — it's called HEAL (Hanson 2015).

It will help you take in the good experiences which help you build resilience and create more lasting feelings of happiness. Sounds pretty great, right? Try it!

Method

1. Have a good experience.
2. Enrich it.
3. Absorb it.
4. Link it.

H — Have a Good Experience

The small ones are just as useful as the big ones here. It could be something small, like a friend said they liked the color of your shirt, or something bigger, like you got nominated to be a peer mentor. It's best to do this in the moment, but you can do it after the fact, too.

Think of one thing that happened in the last 24 hours that made you feel pretty good. Write it or draw a picture of it below.

E — Enrich It

Stay with the good feeling for a little longer than normal, like 10 to 20 seconds. Take a few breaths, and allow yourself to experience feeling good before moving on with your day. So often a good thing happens and we kind of just move on because we're so out of practice with feeling joy. So, in this step, you really grow that good feeling in your body.

A — Absorb It

This is where you get your physical senses involved. Take a moment to visualize the colors, sounds, smells, or tastes associated with it. You can also try to absorb that good feeling in your whole body by doing the following:

1. See if you can identify where in your body you're most feeling the happiness. Maybe there's a little excitement in your chest. Or maybe that spot between your eyes that's always scrunched up in stress now feels a little more relaxed. Maybe you have a giddiness in your belly. Maybe your hands or feet feel light and tingly.
2. Once you've got a good idea of what that good sensation actually feels like in your body, see if you can grow it a little bigger by imagining it spreading throughout your body. Thich Nhat Hanh, Zen master and peace activist, developed an exercise I think of here where you imagine a little smile in the center of your chest spreading bigger and bigger.

L — Link It

Here's the mental contrasting part. But, pay attention here. This part is optional. If you try this out and it crashes that good feeling, then drop this step. You'll still be rewiring your brain to remember more of the positive. You can think of this as a super-adventure-round to try. With this good experience in the foreground of your thoughts, see if you can bring up a related memory that made you feel bad. For example, if your good experience was about someone complimenting your shirt, you can bring up a memory of the time you tried out a new hairstyle and your older sister laughed and asked if it was for Halloween. Keep that good feeling from what you just experienced in the foreground while bringing up that negative experience in the background. See if you can hold both of those in your mind at the same time.

The point is to try to bring up that not-so-good experience, so you can see that it doesn't actually feel so bad now that you can counteract it with a good experience that makes the bad one seem like it wasn't so horrible after all.

Tap into the Power of Physical Senses

When babies are first making sense of the complex world around them, their first instinct is to touch and taste things to learn about them. Before they have language, they can feel, smell, touch, hear, and taste their way through their new world. That's all they need to learn an enormous amount of complex functions and information.

These senses are deeply rooted in your brain, but they aren't given much attention by the time you get to high school. It's way more efficient to have those growing teenage bodies sit and listen quietly while someone tells them the knowledge they need or has them read about it. The alternative is creating something colorful, musical, tactile, or fragrant with it. In no way am I knocking reading and writing as a mode for learning. There's a good reason it's so common. But staying in the same mode over and over again gets boring, which is a state you don't want to be in while learning. So, I'm suggesting here that you approach your schoolwork like an artist by bringing more senses into the mix.

> "[W]henever possible, we should offload information, externalize it, move it out of our heads and into the world" (Paul 2021).

Borrowing from Our Ancient Ancestors

Speaking of artists, there's a reason I think artists have existed in every culture and every time period that I know of, all the way back into ancient times. Before we had the scientific knowledge and advancements we have now, even just the way the sun rose or rain fell from the sky seemed like a super mysterious and uncertain process. In all that uncertainty, our ancestors developed stories and rituals to better explain how the world worked, and so they could feel less lost in it all.

Even with all our scientific knowledge and advancement, life still feels pretty uncertain to most of us at times. I'm not sure there will ever be a point when any one of us will have it all figured out and feel 100 percent certain about how things will go. We won't know the exact "right" path to happiness and success. With all that uncertainty, stories and rituals can still help us remember important information and feel more confident and focused.

Did you know that the amount of information the average American processes on a daily basis in 2011 was five times what it was in 1986? That's a five-time increase just in my lifetime! Not only that, but our brains have a sort of informational speed limit. With it we can't possibly take it all in or properly filter what's most important. A lot will get encoded that we really didn't need, and much will not get encoded that should have been. Structurally, our brains are not all that different from how they evolved during the hunter-gatherer times. Then, an individual might encounter 1,000 people in their lifetime, versus now you'll see that many people just walking through a city or scrolling on your phone in a day. I think this rapid increase of information is sort of like a new wilderness. It is making us feel similar levels of uncertainty and overwhelm that I imagine our ancestors did. So, we're going to need some stories and rituals like our ancestors used to help us clear our minds, soothe our nervous systems, and help our brains filter what's important.

Our ancestors used stories as a way to pass on knowledge and wisdom. Before we had the technology or ability to write things down as a way to transfer knowledge, our ancestors put meaningful information into the format of a story, so it would be easier to remember and pass on through generations. They used things like humor or conflict, vivid elements you could imagine in your mind's eye, to make it visual and emotional. They even added sound elements like rhyme and alliteration so it would stick even more in our brains. That all still works well for us. You'll learn an exercise below for how to apply that to the stuff you need to learn and remember for school.

In addition to story, our ancestors used ritual. Ritual connected our physical senses to help make the unknown and mysterious a little more like something we physically feel. There's a lot you need to learn and remember for school that definitely feels unknown and mysterious. Applying some ritual and physical senses can help you move through it with more ease and success.

Exercise 1: Sense-itive Study Strategies with an Exam Wrapper

In a 2019 study of first year students at Clemson University, students who used exam wrappers "significantly outperform[ed] control students in the course overall." You might be lucky enough to have a teacher who knows this technique and uses it in class. You don't have to leave it up to chance. Just take this worksheet out every time you get a test back and spend 10 minutes filling it out on your own. This exam wrapper helps you plan how to bring more physical senses into your study strategies, so you can study more effectively and feel a little more interested in the whole endeavor, too.

Please note that with this method, the process for studying for your next test starts the day you get your last test back, before you even start learning new material.

Method

1. Fold the wrapper around the test the day you get it back.
2. Spend five minutes reflecting on it.
3. Spend another five minutes planning for the next one.

> **For a reusable version of this exam wrapper,**
> **check out the book bonuses: h2c.ai/hgw**

Fold the Wrapper around the Test the Day You Get It Back

See the wrapper on the following page. Print a copy of this wrapper from the book bonuses online or use a blank template at the end of the workbook. Fold it around the test with the questions facing outward. The front of the wrapper has questions for you to answer and the back is a reference sheet of study strategies that use the physical senses.

Reflect

Take a breath and think kind thoughts to yourself. It can be hard to look back at mistakes, so get yourself a good snack or drink and pretend you're just a non-judgmental scientist collecting facts. If it helps, imagine you're interviewing someone else about it.

NON-JUDGMENTAL POST-TEST CHECK-IN

Grade/score I wanted to get:	
Grade/score I got:	
What parts did I do well on?	
What parts did I miss?	
How many days in advance did I start studying?	
What methods did I use to study?	

Plan for the Next Test

To help you with these questions, be sure to use the handy study method chart for ideas. I want to mention three bonus tips from the research on what really works with studying:

WHAT WORKS WITH STUDYING

1	**Self-testing** This means making something where you can quiz yourself about the information you need to know without looking at the answers. Then check to see if you got it right. All the methods on exam wrapper are easy to turn into tools you can use for self-testing.
2	**Spaced retrieval** This means spreading your studying out into smaller chunks of information to try to remember over time. This helps our brain get it solidly into long-term memory without forgetting it all quickly. You can do this in little bits every day by turning your daily homework into a self-test exercise for 5 to 10 minutes after you finish it. If you don't have daily homework to turn into a quiz, it's usually easy to find a practice quiz on most topics by doing a search on Google, Quizlet, or Khan Academy.
3	**Make your study strategy match the format of the test** For example, if the test is going to be short answer questions, practice writing out answers from memory to questions.

PLANNING FOR THE NEXT TEST

Next test topic		Date	

What do I know about the format of the test?

What materials do I have that would be useful to study?

What methods do I want to use?
See the strategy chart on the next page for help!

What methods do I want to use to study?

4 days before test	
3 days before test	
2 days before test	
1 day before test	

PLANNING FOR THE NEXT TEST

On test day	

How will I remember to take these steps on those days? (Go ahead and set your reminders, write in your planner, or tattoo it on your hand now.)

_____

_____

What other steps can I take to increase my motivation to follow through on this plan?

_____

_____

_____

Sense-itive Self Testing Strategies

STRATEGY	PHYSICAL	VISUAL	AUDITORY	SOCIAL-EMOTIONAL
Make my own practice test.	✓			
Try to rewrite what I know about key terms from memory and check my answers. Keep rewriting the ones I don't know well enough until I get them all.	✓			
Make flashcards with a question on one side and answer on the other. Add a picture to the answers to make it stick.		✓		
Get someone else to quiz me from my notes or the book.			✓	
Get together with a friend and quiz each other or swap practice tests.			✓	✓

STRATEGY	PHYSICAL	VISUAL	AUDITORY	SOCIAL-EMOTIONAL
Put everything I need to know on one page using abbreviations and symbols to make it all fit. Then, try to teach it back to someone else or myself out loud.		✓		
Record myself asking questions, pausing, and then saying the answers. Listen back to it and try to answer the questions during the pause.			✓	
Ask the teacher for help with extra practice problems and questions to practice.			✓	
If I do want to reread my notes, do it after I've already done some self-quizzing and right before I go to sleep at night, so my brain consolidates the information into my memory while I sleep.		✓		
Record a practice test on voice notes. Record a voice note where I ask a question, pause, then say the answer. Then, listen back to it while I'm doing chores, on the bus, walking the dog, etc. Try to answer the question during the pause and then listen to the recorded answer to check myself.	✓		✓	
Hand my daily homework or notes to a parent and have them quiz me from it.			✓	✓
Highlight key terms or definitions in my book or notes. Use a check-set overlay that blocks out the text I highlighted and try to guess the answer.	✓	✓		

Exercise 2: Homework Ritual

Routines are boring, but rituals are interesting. Why? They're mysterious. They're quirky. They involve those powerful physical senses I just went on and on about.

Michael Jordan famously developed a pregame "powder clap" ritual. He'd put chalk on his hands and then clap them over Broadcaster and NBA Icon Jim Kerr, dusting him with it. The ritual was later picked up by Kevin Garnett and LeBron James. If you haven't seen this, you can google it and watch the short video clip of it. You'll see that it has all the essential elements of a good ritual designed to reduce stress and build confidence.

A good ritual should be:

- Filled with physical sensory input (the dust on the hands, the smell of chalk, the sight of it clouding the air)
- Infused with emotion (everyone around including Jordan is laughing about it)
- A little weird and different

Less stress and more confidence is a great formula for happy grades. So let's get to it and design some rituals for two situations when most of you could use the boost in confidence, focus, and motivation: homework and tests.

Method

1. Clear your mind for focus and motivation.
2. Harness time and make a plan.
3. Plan WISE breaks.
4. Plant a pleasant sensory anchor.

Clear Your Mind for Focus and Motivation

Kick off your ritual with an action that helps you focus on the here and now, let go of stress, and gives you a boost of energy. These are usually things that will involve the senses. Here are a three of my favorites:

1. Do a one-minute brain dump (see the bonus strategies in the first section on page 31).
2. Breathe mindfully for three to five minutes. The simplest way to do this is to get comfy, sit or stand tall, and notice your breath coming in through your nose, all the way down into your belly, then back out. Just notice your breath in and out, and if you catch your mind wandering, say to yourself with kind awareness, "Oh! That's what I'm thinking. Focusing back on my breath now."

> I have a lot more ways to relax with mindfulness and **EFT** tapping (an anxiety-relief technique) that I teach in my mindfulness-based stress reduction program. You can find the course on my website: triciaunderwood.com. You can also find a lot of great, free, guided breathing meditations online. I recommend a couple of my favorites for students in the book bonuses.

3. Try a short burst of physical exercise. Pumping your arms up and down really fast twenty times will give you a good surge of energy if you're feeling tired. Put on one of your favorite songs and sing and dance to it. Do a few yoga sun salutations.

Harness Time and Make a Plan

1. Look through all the places that show you what's due.
2. Write down the assignments and steps you need to take today.
3. Strategize and put them in order of first through last. You might need to do a little experimenting to find out what works best for you. Easiest to hardest? Reading first or last? The prevailing wisdom is to get the thing you least want to do out of the way first, but I've seen the opposite work better for some students. It's up to you to see what works best.
4. Take your best guess about how long each step will take and put time estimates next to each one when you want to start them. Include time for breaks.
5. Put this all down on a sticky note, note card, or scratch paper out where you can see it. (Some of my students use a little whiteboard for this because whiteboards are more sensory and fun to use, so it gets them to do this part.)

Plan WISE breaks

Decide ahead of time what you'll do on your breaks and when you want to take them. This keeps you from absentmindedly sliding into distraction rather than relaxation. Here's what I mean by a WISE Break.

	WISE BREAKS
W	**Walk away.** Physically move your body away from the work you were doing. Go to a different room, even outside if you can. This usually has the added benefit of giving your eyes a rest from the blue light of the screen, which more studies are showing has adverse effects on sleep and mental energy.
I	**Invigorate yourself.** Do something to pump energy back into your system. This could be a social interaction, cuddling with a pet, dancing to a good song, or splashing cold water on your face.
S	**Stoppable.** Choose something with a hard stop. Pick something that has a definite end time that is easy to stop when it's over. Scrolling usually doesn't fall into this category. Setting a timer can help.
E	**Empty your mind.** Do something that allows your mind to unwind and clear, instead of getting filled up with new information and stimulation. That friend that always has something dramatic happening is probably not the one you want to call or text right now.

THINGS I COULD DO TO TAKE A WISE BREAK	
1	
2	
3	

Plant a Pleasant Sensory "Anchor" in Your Workspace

Have something in your environment that pleases the senses to help calm your nervous system while you work. This is like an anchor to keep you connected to peace and happiness. Here are some ideas:

- A crystal or smooth stone from a place you love that you can hold in your hand
- A photo of loved ones or a place that makes you happy
- A great smelling candle or oil infuser
- A potted plant — lots of people talk to their plants, and research shows that just looking at something green can lift your mood and relieve stress
- A Post-it of affirmations or turnaround thoughts that send your ANTs running (remember those from Get Peaceful?)

Now put it all together and write out the steps for your personalized homework ritual.

MY HOMEWORK RITUAL	
1	Clear my mind by . . .
2	Plan my tasks and time on (whiteboard, Post-it note, Google tasks, planner page, back of my hand, etc.) . . .
3	I can take WISE breaks by . . .
4	My sensory anchor can be . . .

Almost all these steps can be modified for test
taking as well. Think about how you can modify
your ritual to work for you before tests.

Exercise 3: Story Time

We're sticking with the ancients once again with this section's last practice for getting
sense-itive — storytelling.

Here's a great formula to chart out or summarize a story from any literature class. *Somebody wanted
something. But. So. Then.* Just about every story follows that pattern. A character wants something. That
makes them act and do things. *But*, a conflict happens and things get in their way. *So*, they change or act
again. *Then*, it either works out in the end or not. I bet you can think of just about any show, book, or fairy
tale and apply that formula. In this method, however, we're going to use it to make sense of things that
aren't told as entertaining stories, so you can make what you need to learn more memorable.

Method

1. Imagine the main terms or topics like characters in a story.
2. Get it all in one frame.
3. Retell it.

Imagine the Main Terms or Topics Like Characters in a Story

For practice, think about a topic you are studying. The start of World War I, verb forms, the quadratic
formula, or meiosis will all do. This exercise will make you think about the material in a different way and
stretch your understanding of it. It might be a little hard to come up with the connections at first. But that
stretching feeling is what learning feels like! If it's a little hard to do, that's usually a sign you're doing great,
and your memory of it is going to be even stronger.

You can find a downloadable version at: h2c.ai/hgw

THE CHARACTER(S)	PERSONALITY TRAIT	WHAT DO THEY WANT?	WHAT GETS IN THEIR WAY?	HAPPY OR SAD ENDING FOR THEM?
Phosphorus	It's kind of bland and shy, but with a big surprise when it's alone.	It's highly reactive, so it doesn't want to be around on earth. It's a major boss in the DNA and RNA process to deliver energy.	Deforestation and erosion can make there be too little or too much of it which ruins ecosystems. It wants to be balanced.	Sad ending if we overdevelop natural habitats.

THE CHARACTER(S)	PERSONALITY TRAIT	WHAT DO THEY WANT?	WHAT GETS IN THEIR WAY?	HAPPY OR SAD ENDING FOR THEM?

Here's a fun twist on the storytelling thing: Turn your to-do list into a story. Instead of a to-do list, imagine your day like a scene from a movie. What happens during the beginning, middle, and end that makes it have a happy ending? You can write it as a list but play it in your mind like a story. You can even imagine the conflict that comes up and how the hero (that's you) gets through it. Pick the song that plays in the background when you do it.

Get It All in One Frame by Making a One-Pager

Now, we're going to add another physical sense into the mix: sight. It's so much easier for your brain to remember something it can see all on one page, rather than over pages and pages of notes or piles of flashcards (IRL or on Quizlet). We'll take all that information and put it in a frame. Here are some ideas for creating a one-pager:

- Organize it all into a chart or spreadsheet like the one above. You can use Google Sheets for this. Name the categories across the top and the terms along the side. Here are some category suggestions: What is it? Why is it important? What is it like? What is its opposite?

- Draw a picture of the topic either literally or as an analogy. Label the picture with important terms. Teach it back out loud to someone else, describing the picture and how all the parts relate to each other.
- Condense your notes so they fit on one page. Some of my students love to use a whiteboard for this instead of a piece of paper, so it's easier to erase and move things around. They add symbols, pictures, and arrows to show how things relate, and use different colors for examples or to make key words stand out. Then, they can take a picture of it to review throughout the next day or even right before the test.

> **Here's another example of a one-pager from the Cult of Pedagogy blog (Potash, 2021):**
> **www.cultofpedagogy.com/one-pagers/**

Retell It

Finally, it's time to gather the village around to fire to hear the wisdom that you want to pass along. Okay, maybe it doesn't have to be that elaborate, but the point here is you want to be able to retell your story to make sure you can remember all the information you need. If you try to retell the story and how it relates to what you need to know but can't remember a certain part, that's okay! That just shows you what you need to go back, review, and try again. When you make a mistake like that and then immediately go back to correct it, the neural connection gets even stronger. Retell that story till you're a pro. Oh, and extra points if you can make things catchy with song, rhyme, or physical gestures. At least tell it like you're trying to entertain someone with the tone of your voice. Those are all proven ways to increase the strength of your memory.

Section 3 Reflection

What are the main ideas or points that seem important to you?	Why is something you read about particularly important or relevant to you?
When might you use something you learned?	**Who could you reach out to for help? Can you think of anyone you could help with something you learned?**

P.S. Taking five minutes to fill out a what, who, when, why chart at the end of any section you've read for school is a quick way to make what you read stick. You can always substitute a different question to fit the reading, such as: What were the main points? Who were the most important people involved? When did the important things take place? Why does it matter?

We're moving on now to the fourth pillar. We're almost there! The next section also really plays up the whole sensitive thing. In fact, you might have noticed by now that these four pillars overlap and reinforce each other. It's a lot more like a supportive web than separate pillars. This next section is an excellent way to thread them all together.

GET SENSE-ITIVE KEY TAKEAWAYS

Use your strong emotions to increase happiness and resilience along with your physical senses to improve motivation, focus, and memory.

1	Use RAIN to allow for and deal with negative emotions. Do your best to talk to yourself in kind and nurturing ways.
2	Soak in the good with HEAL. It's not all about dealing with negative emotions. Emotional regulation and resilience is even easier when you take a few extra moments to savor the positive feelings, too.
3	Use mental contrasting to dream optimistically and plan realistically.
4	Bring more senses into your study strategies. Emotion, physical gestures, sights, and sounds all help instill memories stronger and make the whole act of studying a lot more interesting.
5	Create rituals to increase motivation and focus. Our ancestors used rituals to deal with the mysterious and uncertain, and so can you.
6	Use the power of storytelling to remember important information. Stretching your imagination to see the elements you need to learn as a story with characters, conflict, relationships, and action can make it easier to remember.

SECTION 4:
GET SOCIAL

- When you hear the word social, what pictures or images come to mind?
- What strategies do you think you might hear in this section about getting social?

IN THIS SECTION, YOU'LL LEARN ABOUT:

1	**How to use the power of social connection for extroverts**
	Accountability partners
	Peer tutoring and mentorship
	Expressing gratitude
2	**How to use the power of social connection for introverts**
	Being of service
	The magic of co-regulation
	Loving-kindness meditation

Get Social Pep Talk

I'm not sure what came to mind for you when I asked you to think about images related to "getting social." For me I think of a big party scene, and people standing around in circles, talking and laughing in very close proximity to each other. In other words, my nightmare. I'm pretty introverted and always have been. When I was in high school, I sometimes made my mom answer the phone on a Friday night (yes just the one phone we all shared that was connected to the wall with a cord). She told my friends that I was grounded, so I could watch "90210" on the couch alone with my cat. Heaven.

But some of you reading this might be a little or a lot more extroverted. Maybe a party with lots of people to talk to is your version of heaven, and being stuck at home alone on a Friday night sounds like your version of hell. Probably, you're somewhere in between. I have methods in this section for introverts, extroverts, and everything in between.

The truth is we all need at least a little connection with other humans to feel fulfilled and happy. We don't all need the same amount or it in the same kinds of ways, but socializing is proven to lower stress and depression and increase self-confidence and academic success.

Imagine this scene: one person stands at the bottom of a path winding up a hill they're about to climb. They take a deep breath, summon their willpower, and start trudging one foot in front of the other. The next day there are two hikers. They're friends, and one is telling the other a super funny story about the time she went to work with her shirt on inside out (ask me how I know this). Just as they get to the start of the path that winds up the hill, they smile at each other, continue their stride, and barely notice the rise of the path as they walk and talk together.

Researchers at the University of Virginia played out this very scenario. Hikers who stood at the bottom of the hill alone actually judged it to be 30 percent steeper on average than hikers who stood at the bottom of the same hill with a friend.

Our perception of challenge changes when we're around people with whom we feel a positive connection.

The Power of Real Connection

When I was in college, I had a semester when I got depressed. I didn't have the words to describe it at the time, but my grades took a huge dip, which was the only signal to me that something was wrong. By some divine intervention, a professor of mine liked a paper I wrote about Baroque garden art of all things. No one ever said I was one for taking the practical path in life. Anyhow, she asked me to meet with her to talk about presenting it.

What?!? I could barely look at myself in a mirror at that time, never mind getting in front of other people to present my weird theories about 17th century landscape design. She coached me through it. Getting to know her more like a person, one with a family, a messy house, and an office that smelled like the popcorn she ate most afternoons just made me feel better. As you should know by now, when you feel even just a bit better, you start to do better.

When I started having more success in that class, it became easier to put in a little more effort in other classes, too. When I started with a clean slate the next semester, I made it a point to go to my professors' office hours. Hardly anyone took them up on it, and it seemed to make them happy to have a student show some interest. Even though it was a little awkward at first, just showing up and seeing that it usually made them feel good made me feel good as a result. Not only that, but I also found it easier to pay attention in class.

Later, I found out through research that teachers unconsciously provide students who they meet with one-on-one with more verbal and non-verbal cues in class that create subtle, but powerful shifts in how that student then performs. Little things like making more eye contact, a more relaxed or positive tone of voice when addressing them, or the way they would follow up a comment by the student all helped the student learn more effectively. Students would also feel more confident, focus, engage, and retain information from class.

Now, I tell all my high school and college students at the start of a semester that if nothing else, even if they're never going to use a planner or one of our study strategies, make it a point to create a positive one-on-one relationship with your teacher as a human being. It's one of the easiest and most positive ways to raise your grades. It's sort of like a good-hearted Jedi mind trick.

Trading Independence for Interdependence

Even though schools have become much better at working in more opportunities to collaborate with one another, you've probably still received the message to do most of your hard work on your own. This is because we still have a system and culture that tells us getting help is a sign of weakness. One-on-one help is stigmatized as something you only receive if you're already failing (or are about to start). The truth is the most successful people are people who get a lot of help in their lives and also help others. The successful adult version of extra help is called delegating. They have assistants and employees and contractors. They hire housekeepers and success coaches and dog walkers. And all that success means they have more time and influence to help others as well.

I remember when one beacon of success and she-can-do-it-all-ness, Serena Williams, posted about being in a funk adjusting to being a new mom. She said,

> "Talking things through with my mom, my sisters, my friends let me know that my feelings are totally normal" (Garcia 2018).

The Instagram post made waves because of how rare it is to hear an icon who's looked up to for independence and strength share about sometimes needing others to gather strength and resilience. She used those characteristics and talent to win 23 Grand Slam singles titles and hundreds of millions of dollars' worth of brand deals and sponsorships. It wasn't everything needed to feel fulfilled and happy, though. In order to feel truly successful, Williams connects with community. Among other ways she gives back, Williams created the Yetunde Price Resource Center in her home community of Compton, CA. The center provides healing-centered, trauma-informed services to help people who have been affected by trauma to flourish. That's what true success allows — interdependence, being helped by others and giving help back. Do this not because you "should" to look good on a resume, but because it's difficult to feel truly happy or enjoy success without a positive connection with others.

History is filled with stories (unfortunately not always in the history you study at school) of people who overcome obstacles and became so filled with joy, freedom, creativity, and success, that they can't rest until they return those experiences to as many people as they can. It just doesn't feel that good otherwise. We're wired to connect with each other for true thriving. When we take the time to help someone else, like through a process you'll learn about in a few pages called peer tutoring, we have to think a little more clearly about what has worked for us first. This is called metacognition, when you ponder how you think and learn, and it is proven to be a skill that makes academic success a lot more likely (MindShift 2016).

Many of us get the impression that if we achieve a goal or find success by getting help or working together with others, it doesn't "count" as much as if we had done it all on our own. The American culture I grew up with especially loves a story about an individual who climbed to the top all by themselves like Oprah Winfrey, Warren Buffet, and Steve Jobs. However, if you dig deeper, you'll find that they didn't rise without the help and collaboration of other people. In fact, in many of those cases, those people were excellent at building relationships that helped them along the way.

You didn't come here for biographies of the rich and famous. It's important to know that succeeding by connecting with other people is ingrained in your nature, even though it's not usually baked into our working systems, including school. It might take some extra effort to make collaboration happen, since most of our systems don't organize this for you. You'll be working a little against the grain, but it's worth it because connecting with others helps us to grow, expand, and provide mutual support. It can also be for my favorite reason: it just feels good.

Getting Social for Extroverts

> **I encourage you to consider these exercises no matter how introverted or extroverted you feel you are.**

When school shut down due to COVID-19, one of my students, Ben, who had always done pretty well in school, started sleeping through Zoom classes. He was receiving desperate pleas from teachers at the end of the week to turn in something, anything, from his growing list of missing assignments. This behavior to skip, forget, and evade his academics was as much a surprise to Ben as it was to his mother. Rationally, he understood that he was capable of doing the work. He knew that, while COVID-19 was definitely scary, he and his mom were relatively secure and safe, and they would get through this challenge.

So, why was school suddenly a time he could now barely lift his eyelids, never mind his pencil and brain cells? Ben's mother found a big clue on one of the comments she'd gotten about Ben since he was in elementary school at parent-teacher conferences. Ben's teachers consistently remarked on what a kind and courteous kid he was. He'd walk in and say hello and leave class with a "thanks" and "see you tomorrow!" He was the first to lend a hand if something needed to be passed out or picked up and could be relied on to offer himself as tribute when the teacher asked a question no one was venturing to answer.

Ben wasn't a kiss-up or only polite because his mom trained him that way (although she did do an excellent job of that). Ben enjoyed being helpful and having positive relationships with his peers and teachers. Being able to see someone's eyes light up, feel the tension ease in the room, or share a smile when handing a completed assignment to his teacher gave him a boost of dopamine, serotonin, oxytocin, and endorphins that he needed to spark motivation and mental alertness. Without being in-person, a big part of what made him happy in school was shut down. Being social was the fuel that powered up his ability to focus, motivate, and power up the confidence to get through challenges.

One other important thing to know about Ben may resonate with some of you. Ben had an ADHD diagnosis that would often cause him to miss details given in his teachers' verbal directions or skip over a key direction on a handout. However, without even knowing it, he was an expert at gathering clues from the subtle moves of his peers or physical cues from his teacher. In this way he could quickly pick up what was expected of him based on what he was seeing and hearing from his peers.

Realizing this was huge for Ben, right when he was starting to think that there was something deeply wrong with him. It wasn't that. It was that he wasn't being allowed to use something that was deeply right about him. It took some creativity during lockdown but finding small ways to generate genuine social connection involving his schoolwork was an important part of the plan that helped him get back on track. Here are some of the exercises we used that can help you, too, whether you are in person or learning at home.

Exercise 1: **Find an Accountability Partner**

Yep, it's the good ol' buddy system. That might sound like something from elementary school, but there's solid research that proves having partners makes it way more likely that you'll follow through on habits. You reach goals and feel good about yourself while you're at it. The act of simply explaining what you want to do and how you plan to go about it helps you avoid impulsive decisions and gets you back on track quicker if you do happen to slip up.

Method

1. Who to ask
2. How to ask
3. What to talk about

Who to Ask

The best accountability partner has two key ingredients.

HIGH TRUST	LOW STAKES
• This is a person you feel confident will show up and remember when you've committed to check in or meet with each other. • This is also someone who doesn't talk negatively about themselves or other people. How they talk about others gives you a good read about how they might talk about you.	• This is a person who won't hold your mistakes against you. • This is also someone who you won't be tempted to impress or worried about disappointing. ○ For this reason, parents, as much as we love them, are often not the best candidates for this role.

Here is a list to get your wheels turning about who could be a good accountability partner for you:

- A teacher from a past grade who you connected with or liked, but who doesn't teach you now
- A friendly person who works in the school's front office — in my experience at schools, there is always someone who works in the front office who is warm and trustworthy
- Someone in your school's learning or academic resource center — not every school has one of these, but if you're lucky enough to have one that does, take advantage of the great people who work in them (Psst. I used to be one!)
- A cousin, trusted family friend, extended relative like an aunt or uncle, or older sibling who you admire
- A coach or mentor from an extracurricular

List one to three people who could be a good accountability partner for you in the space on the next page.

GOOD ACCOUNTABILITY PARTNERS

1	
2	
3	

If you can't think of anyone, no worries. Hold tight for the next exercise, which can be a good alternative to this one.

How to Ask

Here's a script you can tweak or copy and paste to enlist the help of one of the people you listed above. Make sure to include a bulleted list of topics to cover.

Hi _____!

I'm trying to make some changes, so I can reach some goals I've set for myself. I'm looking for an accountability partner who I can check in with once a week for 15 minutes about my action steps. I have a lot of respect for you, and I'd be so grateful if you could help me with this.

If you're up for it, just reply and let me know the most convenient way and times for you to touch base. I'm including some suggested topics (see bulleted list below) we could cover in our meetings, but I'm also up for any suggestions you have, too! Looking forward to hearing back from you and hope you are well.

Signed,

_____

What to Talk About

Here are some suggested topics to cover during your meetings with your accountability partner.

SUGGESTED DISCUSSION TOPICS	
Goals	Write down a long-term goal in your planner or notes on your phone. It should be something you want to achieve in the next one to six months that is a little bit of a stretch, but doable, and that would make you happy about life. If you want, you can also relate this to an even bigger dream you have for yourself far off in the future.
Wins	What worked well last week? Grades? How many times did you follow through on your habit this past week? Look back at your weekly plan from last week. Are you satisfied with how you completed those plans? When you think about the week ahead, what do you want to list as your wins then?
Misses	What didn't work out the way you planned or wanted? Is there anything you can do next week to avoid that from happening again? What obstacles keep getting in your way?
Plans	What are all the things that need your time and attention in the week ahead? Map that out in a weekly planner or schedule. Then, break down the best way for you to prepare for each one without last minute stress.
Habits	What are one to five everyday behaviors you want to make a habit to help you reach your goal? Think about obstacles here. What habits might make those obstacles less likely to get in your way?
Check-ins	Decide if it's a good idea for your accountability partner to check in with you via text or email about your progress during the week.

Exercise 2: Peer Tutoring/Mentorship

Several studies show that students learn more easily from people who are closer to them in age. And since I'm not getting any younger, this is very good news. In addition, students who serve as a mentor or tutor for other students boosts their metacognition skill I mentioned earlier. They end up getting better grades without directly trying, because helping others helped their personal levels of happiness and academic self-confidence.

Methods

1. Get a peer tutor.
2. Be a peer tutor.
3. Start a peer tutoring program.

Get a Peer Tutor

If your school has a peer tutoring program, sign up to get one. Peer tutors know how to explain things in ways you haven't heard before and in terms that might be way more relatable than an adult would use. Often, they've had the same teacher and can tell you some little tricks about what that teacher most wants to see from you in class and in your work. That way you can focus your energy on the details that matter most and not on the things that won't make a big difference. They will have figured out the best resources for studying and have probably figured out a thing or two about the best study methods for that particular class. It's encouraging to meet with someone who has been in your shoes before.

Be a Peer Tutor

If your school has a peer tutoring program, sign up to be one. You don't have to be a straight-A student to serve as a peer tutor. I found that the peer tutors who had the greatest effect on others were ones who didn't have a super easy time in a certain class, but had made some progress by the end of the course. It's hard to explain how to do something to someone else when you're a natural at it. If you're just a little further down the road, you can use your experience to help inform another student on what to expect. Add some tricks and tips that worked for you and a couple suggestions about how to get unstuck for when they feel stuck. You'll be surprised at how good it makes you feel and how much more confident about your own competence as a student you'll get.

Start a Peer Tutoring Program

If your school doesn't have a peer tutoring program, start one. In the spirit of "the small things are the big things," you can start small here. Approach a teacher in a class you are struggling with the work. Ask them if they know of any students who they think might be willing (and good at) helping you with the assignments or studying. Usually, teachers love to see students taking initiative like that, and they'll be happy to help you find someone. Likewise, you can ask a teacher in a subject that you think you can help others if they know of any students who could use your help. You can find a couple handy resources for getting a peer tutoring program started in your school in the book bonuses.

Exercise 3: Express Gratitude

Even though most of us were taught when we were young to say "thank you" to be polite, hardly anyone teaches gratitude as a method for raising your grades at school, but it does! Here's why.

Expressing appreciation increases feelings of closeness and strengthens connections with others. This gives you a two-for-one boost that helps you do better in school because:

1. Those feelings of closeness are a result of extra serotonin and oxytocin in your nervous system, which helps lower stress and improve things that really help in school like focus, memory, and self-efficacy.

> **Self-efficacy means having confidence in your own abilities and believing you have the power to accomplish things in different areas of your life. It's about recognizing your strengths and skills. It's also trusting yourself to handle challenges and achieve your goals.**

2. The strong connections increase the network of people who are willing to offer support, help, encouragement, and opportunities to you. You will have a stronger support network around you, and that helps you feel more confident to tackle bigger challenges.

Method

1. Show it.
2. Tell it.
3. Write it down.

Show It

Offer help to people you appreciate without being asked. Small, helpful gestures like cleaning up the dishes at home or lending a hand to pick up after a class activity show the people you appreciate that you notice their hard work and don't take it for granted.

In class, show gratitude by showing your attention with body language. When someone is attentive, they sit up, lean forward a little, smile at the jokes, ask questions, and offer comments when prompted. Even if you're bored, acting like you're listening to the greatest speech ever given shows the teacher you are grateful for them showing up and sharing something they obviously like. Most of the time they'll notice and appreciate you back for it.

Tell It

Here are three small actions you can make a habit to get big results:

	WAYS TO TELL IT
1	Say thank you, preferably with eye contact and a smile, to your teachers when you leave class. Experiment with doing this every day for a month. Track the difference it makes in your attention, motivation, and how the teacher treats you in class.
2	Set a reminder at the end of each month to write an email or even an actual letter to someone in your life who you appreciate and tell them why.
3	Wear a rubber band or string around your wrist to remind you to look for something someone does that day that you appreciate. Don't forget to tell them why you appreciated it. So, instead of just saying "thanks" if you see the custodian cleaning up a mess in the hallway, give it a little more meaning with detail. Say something like, "Thanks for keeping the hallway clean. It makes me feel less stressed out when things are clean."

Write It Down

Gratitude journals work. You don't need a fancy, leather-bound diary to do this. Write down three to five things every day that make life enjoyable. It can be as big as winning an award or as small as feeling the sun on your skin. The real fun part about this is that you will start to look for and notice more of those enjoyable moments throughout the day. It starts to feel like it's magically bringing in more things to enjoy in your life, when really it's all part of that reticular activating system we learned about back in Get Peaceful.

GUIDE TO GRATITUDE JOURNALS

Where to write it	I just love tiny notebooks, so I get a pack of tiny notebooks and keep them on my nightstand. It really doesn't matter where you write it. There are apps like 365 Gratitude if you'd rather go the digital route. Either way, I highly recommend you physically write or type it out.
When to do it	Attach it to something you already do every day. I recommend making this part of your bedtime ritual. It's a pleasant way to train your mind for more positive thoughts before sleeping.
How to supercharge it	Writing down three to five things is enough to get the benefits, but to really amp it up, try picking just one. As you bring it to mind, breathe mindfully in and out three times. Notice what that gratitude feels like in your body. Where do you feel it? What does that feel like? If it helps, you can use these mindfulness prompts I learned from one of my favorite mindfulness teachers for teens, Dzung X. Vo: "Breathing in I know this is gratitude. Breathing out I smile. Gratitude… Smiling…" (The Mindful Teen, Vo, 2015).

Getting Social for Introverts

I am a classic introvert. I love my alone time and get overwhelmed and exhausted when I have to mix it up with a crowd of people. I enjoy close relationships with just a few select friends and family members, and that seems to be all I need to feel socially fulfilled. With this in mind, I want to promise you that there are ways to generate the benefits of social connection without needing to go against your nature. Maybe because I am one, I love introverts and their influence in our world, so I'm not trying to change that.

> "The secret to life is to put yourself in the right lighting. For some, it's a Broadway spotlight; for others, a lamplit desk. Use your natural powers — of persistence, concentration, and insight — to do work you love and work that matters. Solve problems. Make art. Think deeply" (Cain 2012).

Alyssa was the kind of student who always received this kind of comment on her reports from teachers, "I encourage Alyssa to participate more. I know she has interesting insights and would like to hear more of them in class." Through the years, Alyssa grew to accept that she was better off not trying too hard to get in with the rest of her verbose peers to offer comments and questions. Usually summoning the effort to do so distracted her, and she would lose focus. Instead she learned to participate and grow in social connection in ways that were in alignment with her nature rather than against it.

She created *sketchnotes* of the class discussion that demonstrated how tuned in she was to her peers' reflections. The teacher got her to share them with her classmates to help everyone remember the key points from class. Alyssa also tapped into one of her interests by joining the urban farming club at school. There, she got to connect with others over a shared interest in hands-on projects rather than just hanging out and talking, which always seemed to make her feel awkward and depleted afterwards. Joining the urban farming club also helped her build confidence and develop her leadership skills in her own way.

> **Sketchnotes are a visual way of taking notes that combines text with simple drawings and doodles. Instead of writing long sentences or paragraphs, you use icons, symbols, and diagrams to represent key ideas and concepts. There are abundant free sketchnote tutorials on the internet. They would be a good way to use some summer break time to learn about and practice.**
>
> **Bonus points: sketchnote your summer reading book or a topic you know is in store for you next semester.**

Doing nice things for others is a proven way to boost the feel-good chemicals in your nervous system like dopamine, serotonin, oxytocin, and endorphins. They help you reduce stress and increase feelings that are helpful for reaching your goals like motivation, confidence, and self-efficacy.

All the exercises below are related to *empathy*, something many introverts do well. It means being in tune with the emotions of others, an ability to accurately imagine and understand what others are thinking or feeling. In fact, that strength could be the reason why introverts don't like to be as outgoing and social in big groups. It's overwhelming to be so attuned to all those emotions and feelings all around you. The good news is that empathetic strength is also highly correlated to academic achievement when you learn how to use it.

Below are some additional ways you can get the benefits of social engagement while still honoring your introverted nature.

Exercise 1: Be of Service

We're biologically wired as a species to be kind to others because we're essentially pack animals — yes, even you, wallflower. It helps us survive and thrive together. In our busy lives today, it's easy to forget that natural instinct. I'm going to show you a few ways to keep it top of mind and work it easily into your everyday life. You reap the benefits when you relate to others positively, strengthen empathy, and create a strong support network of people around you.

Methods

1. Start with yourself
2. Small acts of kindness for others
3. Community kindness

Start with Yourself

Be extra kind to yourself. When you catch yourself in a moment of self-criticism or doubt, talk to yourself like you would to a good friend. Use second and third person like this: "You are going to be okay. Laurie, yep, you made a mistake, but guess what? You're human, and you can totally recover from this."

That's how to be kind to yourself in the moment. You can also be kind to future you by answering these questions:

What's a situation that always seems to cause stress or hiccups? (Rushing and being late in the mornings is a common one for a lot of my students.)

	How can I prepare something in advance that would be nice to a future me who could use the boost during one of these stressful situations?
Examples:	lay your clothes out the night before, put some ingredients together to make your favorite smoothie easy to grab and go, set a favorite song to play when you wake up in the morning, etc.

Small Acts of Kindness for Others

You can also do very small things throughout your day to be kind to both friends and strangers. Here are some ideas:

- Hold a door open for someone.
- Bake something or make art (or some other creative endeavor you like to do for fun).
  - Give it to someone who would appreciate it — a neighbor, your lunch buddy, a teacher, or a member of the school support staff who seems a little frazzled and could use some kindness.
- Give someone a compliment.
- Smile at a teacher when you walk into or out of their classroom.
- Wear a string or rubber band around your wrist to remind you to do one small act of kindness each day.

Community Kindness

Find a group in school or your community that volunteers and join them. Volunteering alongside other people is a great way to get social for those of us who don't love to make small talk and mingle at parties. If this is interesting to you, google local volunteer opportunities for teens right now. You can check and see if your school has a volunteer or community engagement coordinator. I'm willing to bet if you asked an adult, a counselor, advisor, or teacher at your school about volunteer opportunities, they'd jump at the chance to help you find one. Write down one to three results of your search for ways to engage in community kindness below.

WAYS TO ENGAGE IN COMMUNITY KINDNESS	
1	
2	
3	

Exercise 2: Tap into the Magic of Co-regulation

Co-regulation is the power one person's emotional state has to change the emotional states of those near them. It's the scientific term explaining why emotions and behaviors are contagious. If you are around someone who is really stressed, it also makes you feel a little more stressed. It works in the opposite way as well. If you are around someone who is energetic, focused, calm, or motivated, it also rubs off on you. Technically, it isn't due to some kind of magic, mind-melding power. Science explains that it has to do with the way the mirror neurons in our brains read non-verbal cues, like tone of voice and body language. It then signals to our nervous system to feel similarly so we fit the emotion. The neuroscience on it is fascinating. You don't have to read about the science right now, you can run your own experiments to try it out for yourself.

Methods

1. Co-regulating with strangers
2. Co-regulating with friends
3. Co-regulating all by yourself

Co-regulating with Strangers

Make a plan to do some of the academic work you feel most unmotivated to tackle somewhere where other people are working. Go to the library, a classroom of a teacher you like, or a coffee shop. See if you can get your parents to set up an hour or so of co-working time together at the table. (But only if they promise not to look over your shoulder and try to do your work with you. They should bring their own quiet work to do.)

Think of three places right now where you can go to work around other people who are focused and motivated.

PLACES WHERE OTHERS ARE FOCUSED AND MOTIVATED	
1	
2	
3	
How can you make working at one of these places a part of your weekly routine? Are there any steps you need to take to make that happen?	

Co-regulating with Friends

When you're coming up on a test or big project, plan to avoid being around classmates who are always talking about how stressed or worried they are about it.

Create a study group or make a plan with a friend or two to get homework done at the same time. Preferably do this in the same place together, but Zoom or FaceTime works, too, if that makes it more possible.

Co-regulate All by Yourself

If you can trust yourself with YouTube during homework or study time, try out the "Study With Me" YouTube channel at www.youtube.com/@TheStriveStudies. At my last count, there were 345,000 subscribers who were enjoying the effect co-regulating has on increasing their ability to be calm and focused. Watch how she settles in to work, reads, and takes notes quietly in structured times for deep focus and short breaks. Work alongside her.

Exercise 3: Loving Kindness Meditation

Although this meditation practice has been around for centuries, new research keeps proving how powerful it is.

> "A growing body of research has been examining the effects of this [meditation] practice on the brain and body, such as improved positive mood and feelings of well-being, as well as the improved ability to take the perspective of someone else, which is needed for positive social emotions…This practice increases our sense of connection and reduces loneliness" (Jha 2021).

Meditation increases feelings of social connection without even having to be with another person in the moment. On top of that, it decreases negative emotions, harmful negative self-criticism, and negative bias against others. It's a simple, easy, and powerful supercharge to your happiness and success. This one is a definite winner.

Method

1. Clear your mind and relax.
2. Do three "loving kindness rounds."
3. Savor the good feelings.

Clear Your Mind and Relax

Sit comfortably. Reassure yourself that you are doing something important for your well-being and goals. There is nothing else you need to do or think about for the next five minutes. Breathe deeply. Notice your breath coming in and filling your body. Then breathe out and notice your breath going out. Do this for another breath or two until you feel relaxed.

Do Loving Kindness Rounds

1. Think of a person or pet who makes it easy to feel happy when you think of them. Get a picture of them in your mind. With a gentle smile on your face, say these words to them silently:

> **May you be happy.**
>
> **May you be healthy.**
>
> **May you be safe.**
>
> **May you have peace.**

2. As you give them these warm wishes, your heart may feel full. You may not feel that, and that's okay, too. I like to imagine those wishes radiating out to them, and I see them getting a little boost of happiness without knowing why.
3. Now, let the picture of them go. Bring to mind a person that who you feel neutral about. It can be someone you don't have much of a connection with, but you see them around. Go through the same phrases with a gentle smile on your face. Wish them well in the same way.
4. Next, call up a sense or image of yourself. Repeat those phrases to yourself with the same feeling of goodwill.
5. Finally, move on to everyone in your school, home, neighborhood, city, and country, until you include all beings everywhere. Visualize the whole of that place or even the Earth and then offer those phrases to everyone there.

During the practice, you can notice when your mind wanders off to other thoughts — it probably will — and gently guide your attention back to it.

Savor It

When you're done, if you're like me, you might feel a gentle feeling of happiness or love in your body. You can take a few more moments to breathe. Let that good feeling stay before you move on with your day. Know you can come back to that feeling by taking a few mindful breaths.

If you liked the way that felt, then it's a win in the short term and the long term. You get a few minutes of feeling peaceful and happy, and the research shows that it has long-lasting benefits for your physical and mental health way into your future. A few times a week really amplifies the power of it.

Section 4 Reflection

Here's a quick review of the points we covered in this section:

FOR EXTROVERTS	FOR INTROVERTS
Accountability partners	Be of service
Peer tutoring/mentorship	Use the magic of co-regulation
Express gratitude	Loving kindness meditation

Remember, these labels are just suggestions. In reality these strategies can work for any type of person, so use the strategy that feels best rather than going by a label.

What are the main ideas or points that seem important to you?	Why is something you read about particularly important or relevant to you?
When might you use something you learned?	Who could you reach out to for help? Can you think of anyone you could help with something you learned?

P.S. Taking five minutes to fill out a what, who, when, why chart at the end of any section you've read for school is a quick way to make what you read stick. You can always substitute a different question to fit the reading, such as: What were the main points? Who were the most important people involved? When did the important things take place? Why does it matter?

Well, we've made it through all four pillars! Take a cue from Get Playful and do your mini celebration for this win. It's a big deal to read through a whole self-improvement book. It shows your commitment and the level of trust you can now have in your ability to make a difference in your own life. Before we wrap things up, I've snuck in one more little bonus section. It's not a pillar so much as a foundation I've used in my career to find ways to help students who weren't thriving in a one-size-fits-all school system. It helped them find their own way to happiness and success. Maybe I should've started with the foundation, but in true rebel fashion, I've turned it all upside down and am including it here at the end. In fact, being critical of doing things the "normal" or "traditional" way is pretty much the theme of this last section. Read on to see this final useful mindset: get countercultural.

GET SOCIAL KEY TAKEAWAYS

Cultivating ways to connect positively with others boosts the qualities we need for happiness and success.

1	Find and use an accountability partner. They can help you stay motivated and keep your focus on habits and goals for success.
2	Get involved in peer tutoring. Being helped and helping others improves confidence and metacognition, two key factors for success.
3	Express gratitude. This increases feel-good chemicals in your nervous system to reduce stress and improve mental energy.
4	Be of service. Helping alongside others is a great way to feed your need for social connection when you're a bit shy about striking up conversation with others.
5	Use the magic of co-regulation. Our mental and emotional states are contagious. Get yourself around others who are feeling the way you would like to feel to give your focus and positivity a boost.
6	Meditate on loving-kindness. If you'd like to improve relationships, feel happier, and lower stress, this is one of the most feel-good, easy ways to do it.

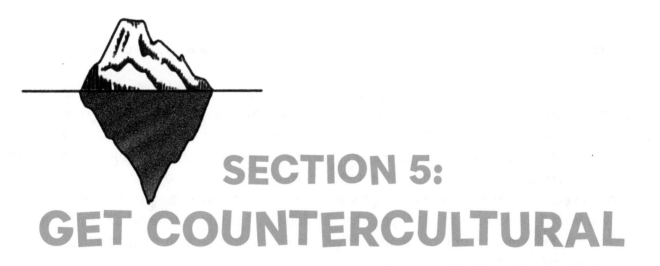

SECTION 5:
GET COUNTERCULTURAL

- What are some things about "the way things are" in school and society that really bug you and just don't seem right?
- Who do you see that is being left out or not benefiting from the way things are?
- What are some strengths, interests, and talents you have that you don't see being valued or included that much in school or society?

Get Countercultural Pep Talk

Fortunately, I have never been one to do things the traditional way. My mind just doesn't work like that.

I say "fortunately" now, but for most of my life, I thought that was unfortunate. It meant that school assignments would take me longer to read and complete, and my grades didn't reflect my efforts. I was dissatisfied as a teacher with the way schools operated. I had a hard time only "doing my job" without sticking my nose into lots of other places to try to make the system different for my students and myself. For a long time, I doubted the way I thought and felt and worked. I thought of myself as somehow missing something everyone else had. Everyone being those who were better able to go with the flow.

If you feel a little like that too, my hope is that you don't have to take as long as I did before realizing that there is nothing missing or broken inside of you. You might just be a bit countercultural, which is actually a great thing that we need in this world.

To me, being countercultural doesn't mean being against everything for the sake of it all the time. That makes you grumpy — a state of mind I'm hoping this book helps you have less often. Instead, I believe being countercultural means you don't just accept things because that's the way everyone else is doing them. Maybe you like to think a little more deeply about things. Or maybe you have an inner voice that's always asking why things are the way they are:

- Why is this set up this way?
- Who benefits from it being this way?
- Who is not benefiting from it being this way?
- Why is it like this?
- How could this be even better?
- Is anyone being left out?
- Is there anything about the way this whole thing works that just doesn't sit right with me? Why?

It's that last question that led me down the interesting and fulfilling path to what I do now: creating things that help more and more teenagers find their own unique power to handle school with more happiness and success.

What began as a choice to find a career that was less boring than an office job led me to teaching high school. And did I ever get what I asked for in that situation. In addition, I had a lot of opportunities to question things that didn't sit right with me.

Martha Beck, one of my favorite mentors and teachers, taught me to really listen when my emotions or body seems to be saying, "Wait, this can't be right." It's a sense or feeling that comes up any time something is going on that takes you away from living in peace — the way we're meant to live. I think a whole successful future and great life can be built off paying attention to that feeling and figuring out one small action at a time to move toward what feels better. Throughout your life, experiment with how to make that thing that just doesn't seem to be quite right a little bit better for yourself and others.

The reason why that's countercultural is because our culture says things like this about some of the feelings you get that might not feel quite right:

WAIT, THAT CAN'T BE RIGHT	CULTURE SAYS. . .
I dread doing homework.	Suck it up and power through it!
I'm exhausted.	What doesn't kill you makes you stronger. Go big or go home!
There's so much stuff to do — I'm overwhelmed!	You just need to get more organized.
This is boring.	It'll be important for you to know this stuff later.
I feel like I have to be perfect to be successful at school.	It's getting harder and harder to get into college. Work hard now, so you can crush the competition. You can relax later.
I worked hard for that test and still didn't get a good grade.	Your GPA determines your success in life. You better find a way to fix it!

Hopefully, *Happy Grades* has helped you see things in a different way than what mainstream school culture says. Something more like this:

WAIT, THAT CAN'T BE RIGHT	BUT YOU SAY. . .
I dread doing homework.	How can I bring a little more fun and joy into this?
I'm exhausted.	That means I need to take a break to breathe, connect with a friend, go for a walk outside, journal about how I feel and what I want, or help someone else out. I know how to take care of myself and slowing down to do that will help me more in the long run than getting everything done quickly.
There's so much stuff to do — I'm overwhelmed!	I can get some help to figure out my best next step.
This is boring.	Let me put a little more of my style into this to make it better. What can I relate this to that I like or already know about? Who can I do this work with who might make it more fun and interesting?

WAIT, THAT CAN'T BE RIGHT	BUT YOU SAY...
I feel like I have to be perfect to be successful at school.	I get to feel happy and be successful even when I'm imperfect. I can make mistakes — just like every human out there — learn from them, and keep growing. There is no perfect, even for those who have all their honors and boxes checked. I can always make things better a little bit at a time, even if that means being patient and reaching out to someone I trust for help.
I worked hard for that test and still didn't get a good grade.	Success is the happiness you feel when you're working toward your potential. I get to see mistakes as useful information and enjoy the process of trying something different next time. Whether I get a good grade or not, I get to enjoy how it feels to get creative, try again, and do my best.

I know none of the things in that second list seem like big dramatic ways to overturn systems that destroy the Earth and continue cycles of violence and oppression against people based on race, class, and gender. But you know that I believe the small things are the big things. Acting in this way might eventually lead you to some pretty big, excellent, magnificent outcomes in your life, solve gnarly problems from your unique perspective, and create more opportunity for others. In fact, I wouldn't have written this whole darn book for you if I didn't think it would.

I'm going to tell you about two big myths about success that I see get in my students' way. Then I'll give you a few exercises for getting countercultural with them.

Myth 1: Dream it, Do it

If you know much about me, you can probably guess I'm a big fan of dreaming. In fact, I think of myself as sort of an expert in the field because I do it so often. Saying that "dream it, do it" is a myth isn't to say that dreaming is bad for you, and you should get real and just be practical all the time. I believe in this myth, actually. Dreaming is necessary for creating a great life for yourself. The myth part is that if this formula doesn't seem so simple to you, there's something wrong. That isn't true. There's a lot of trial and error that goes on in that comma between dream it and do it. I want to share a few exercises that might take some of the errors out of all that trial for you, so you can dream like a pro.

I can tell you from personal experience and research that there are a few places where dreaming can lead us astray. We can dream things we think we want, only to find out that they don't satisfy us as much as we hoped because it was actually someone else's dream for us. Or we can get fired up about a dream that we just thought we should want because we saw others looking so happy with it, when in reality they weren't as happy as they looked. Before we proceed to the "do it" part of dreaming it, I want to make sure you have achieved an expert level of dreaming.

Your Body Is Part of the Thinking Process

We tend to think dreaming happens in the mind, but our bodies are great sources too. They tell us when our dreams are really coming from our truth versus from what someone else wants for us or what we've been duped by marketing to want. Dreams that are about what we truly want for ourselves are invigorating.

> And, you guessed it, here comes my last word-nerd moment in the book. The root of invigorate is vigor, which means energy or force. Something that invigorates fills your body with physical energy. Without good rest and physical exercise, that physical signal could get missed by a run-down body experiencing feelings of depression, stress, and lack of focus.

Besides helping us to read our physical signals about what's true and right for us, the research shows that taking really good care of our bodies ends up being an even stronger predictor of things you probably want in your dreams like good grades, a well-paying job, positive relationships, and happiness.

Once you do have a dream, we're often told to go after it with everything we have. Movies are filled with heroes who sacrifice sleep and physical well-being to save the world or reach their dream. The truth is, chronic personal sacrifice and exhausting yourself makes it less likely you'll achieve what you want in life. So, once you have a clear dream for yourself, prioritize taking great care of your body as one of the most important things you can do to reach your dream.

The Pitfall of Comparison

Another pitfall of dreaming is comparison. Sometimes the "dream it, do it" myth gets exaggerated in the media, social and otherwise, by making it look like the success and happiness of others was an easy, meteoric rise to the top. With so many influencers looking happy and wildly successful (and with good hair while they're at it), comparison can make you feel like you must be doing something wrong if you don't have their same level of success or at least don't look as cute while you're trying. Psychological research proves that we overestimate how happy and put together others are and underestimate the challenges they're going through. This is especially true on social media when we're comparing others' outside appearances to how we feel on the inside. It's an unfair comparison. Yes, the social media companies are extorting and profiting off of this psychological weakness of ours, and I wish they'd quit it, but the truth is your brain will still find ways to compare yourself to others IRL, too.

Teenagers are especially practiced in comparison. It's an important part of how you form your identity at this age. Comparing yourself to others helps you decide what kind of person you want to be. The area of your brain that compares you to others around your same age is especially active right now. You know all about the negativity bias now, so you can guess that your brain is usually not doing all that comparing from a gentle, kind, or even neutral place. Usually, comparing ourselves to others can lead us to putting ourselves down, feeling insecure, and feeling unmotivated in our attempts to improve our lives. Psychologists have given it a cute rhyming name, I guess to make us feel better about it: the compare-despair cycle.

There's no use in me telling you to "stop comparing yourself to others." It's just wired into your neurobiology right now, and I don't yet have the political influence to get social media companies to quit capitalizing on this fragile aspect of our psychology, either. So, if you're going to do it, maybe I can help you do it in a way that helps rather than hurts your success and happiness.

Non-attachment

We're going to apply a mindfulness technique to our dreams — *non-attachment*. That means that you go ahead and allow your dreams to get you all fired up to take focused action, but then you let go of your expectation about the outcome of your action. If that seems contradictory, it is, but in a good way. Mindfulness, just like life, is full of those kinds of contradictions. Attaching your self-worth to the outcome of your effort just puts a whole lot of unhelpful pressure on you through the process. Here are two stories to illustrate that point.

Striving for an A

Imagine Jane really wants to get an A on a test. She dreams about that result. She imagines the pride she'll feel when she gets that grade back, and the confidence in knowing how she handled her business and got it done. That makes her feel inspired, so she starts taking action to make it happen. A full week ahead she lays out and organizes all the materials she has that can help her study.

She really wants this to work, so she stays up late that night making flashcards. She skips exercising and seeing her friends that week so she can do practice tests and reread her notes. The lack of rest or activities that make her feel relaxed and happy makes it easier for stress to settle on Jane. Now she feels like she needs to get that grade in order to make this all worth it. The exhaustion makes her start doubting that she has what it takes. Rather than inspiring her, this whole process of studying is starting to feel terrible. But she pushes on because so much is riding on getting the result she wants.

On test day, she finds that the test has questions on it she didn't expect, so she feels crushed and angry at the unfairness of it all. She thinks the teacher is trying to trip her up on purpose. She gives up trying to apply what she studied to the questions, since it probably won't matter anyway. And, long, tragic story short, Jane ends up getting a B– on the test — about the same grade she has been getting all along. This whole endeavor felt awful and didn't produce the results she wanted, so she decides it wasn't worth it. She believes she's just not the type of person who can do well on tests.

Well, that's a sad story, isn't it? Because the title of this book is *Happy Grades*, let's rewrite that story using non-attachment. It starts in the same place. Jane has an inspiring dream to get an A on the test. And she uses all that inspiration to formulate a plan and take inspired action a week ahead of time just like before. But then, she does something a little different.

A Happier Ending

Using non-attachment, Jane lets go of the outcome of the A as the goal. That would be great, but she instead believes what's most important is that she acts like the kind of person who gets the A: proud, determined, focused, and confident. As long as she acts like that kind of person during the process, she can be proud of herself, no matter what the result turns out to be. She makes the flashcards but takes breaks so she can recharge and keep her focus. She makes sure she gets to bed at a good hour each night, so she's well rested. She makes plans with her most positive friends and even does some studying with them the night before the test. She didn't do all the practice tests she hoped to because she wanted to go to rock climbing, which always helps with her confidence and feeling clear-headed. So that night after practice, when she rereads her notes, she comes up with a brilliant idea to condense them into a one-pager. She carries that one pager around with her and pulls it out during those slivers of time when she's waiting in line for lunch or waiting for her teacher to start class.

On test day, she's rested, clear headed, and confident. She has no regrets about how she spent her time and is proud of herself already for making positive changes in her approach. She's surprisingly excited to see what the test is like and how she'll do. It feels like a game to play. She notices the trick questions and sure, it makes her stumble a bit. She remembers what a tutor once told her if that happens — do what you can, go on to an easier question, then go back to it. That works with a couple of the questions but not with all of them. She ends up getting a B+ on the test. Better than her previous test grades, but not quite the outcome she dreamt about. However, the process felt like a positive one. She can see and feel how she made progress, so she wants to keep it up and try again for the next test. Much happier ending, right? Read on to find out more about how to use non-attachment for your dreams too.

Exercise 1: Take Good Care of Your Body

This exercise isn't about having a healthy body to look good or to impress your doctor at your next physical. This is about making sure that your GPS, or more accurately, your PGS — Personal Guidance System — is in working order. Our physical bodies are an excellent source of wisdom for helping us know what feels right and wrong. It hints what dreams are right for us and which ones are really about someone else or a trick of marketing and cultural pressure. Our bodies also give us the energy to move in the direction of our dreams with power and ease. So, let's give them what they need to be great Personal Guidance Systems for us.

Method

1. Give it sleep and rest.
2. Move it around.
3. Be aware of it.

Give It Sleep and Rest

Below is a chart so you can figure out how to get better sleep based on what we know is the best kind of sleep. Remember, we're not going for perfection here, just small improvements. Rate each on a scale of 1 to 10 with 1 being "I am nowhere near this standard" and 10 being "I do this just about everyday."

SLEEP IS BEST WHEN IT'S...	
1	**Regular and at nighttime** Napping or catching up on the weekends doesn't have the same positive results for your brain as sleeping at night at consistent times.
2	**Between seven and nine continuous hours**
3	**Distanced from your screens** Not being exposed to the blue light, stimulation, and stress from social media and phone or computer screens an hour before sleep improves sleep quality. It improves even more when you sleep in a different room from your phone, even when it's on silent.

BEST SLEEP PARAMETERS	CURRENT RATING	10% BETTER GOAL
Regular and at nighttime		
Between seven and nine continuous hours		
Distanced from my screens		

Move It around

For the purpose of this book, aka improved happiness and success at school, exercise isn't about getting super physically fit. It's about giving your nervous system a dose of natural feel-good chemicals that improve mood and *cognition* (your ability to think clearly).

When would be the best time to get 20 to 30 minutes of physical movement into my day on most days?	

What kinds of physical activity do I enjoy or suspect I might enjoy?	

Which of the following options can I choose to make it even more likely that I'll follow through with this? (Check the ones you choose to the left of the option.)	
	Make a public commitment. Tell someone I know that I intend to do it.
	Add some music or something else I enjoy listening to.
	Get a friend to join me.
	Reward myself every time I do it. Remember to keep the reward easy, simple, and healthy. A sticker or hug from a loved one will do!
	Block it out in my schedule like it's an important meeting I have to attend. Set a reminder for it.
	Join a team, club, or class.
	Other:

Be Aware of It

To know when our bodies are trying to tell us something important, it's great to get into the practice awareness. We want to be aware of how our bodies feel in the present moment. The body scan practice is one of my students' favorites because it has the added benefit of relieving stress.

Let's try that now:

1. Get comfortable. Either sit or lie on your back.
2. Notice your breath. Feel it moving in and out of your body.
3. Scan each part of your body with your breath from your feet up to the top of your head. Imagine you're breathing into each body part. Imagine what the space in that part feels like as you inhale. Imagine it getting more open and relaxed as you exhale.
4. When you're done, bring awareness to your body as a whole. Breathing in, imagine your breath moving into every part of your body. Breathing out, imagine a smile spreading from the inside out to your face.

> **You might find it helpful to do this with guided audio first. My favorite guided audio body scan can be found for free at www.mindfulnessforteens.com/guided-meditations**
>
> **You can find plenty of others on YouTube by searching "body scan meditation."**

Exercise 2: Turn Compare and Despair into Compare and Care

Since you're programmed for comparison — it's part of the deal with being born a pack animal — let's try doing it for your own good. As you read about earlier, we all have a tendency to use everyone else's absolute best as our reference point for how we should be doing in our normal, everyday life. It's not an accurate reference point and can lead to depression, anxiety, and low self-confidence. You'll learn here how to change your reference points so when you do compare, you're left feeling inspired and motivated instead of disheartened.

Method

1. Write a letter to the object of your comparison.
2. Use yourself as your reference point.
3. Manage your social media use.

Write a Letter to the Object of Your Comparison

> **Write a positive note to someone you see as "better" than you. Tell them all about what you like about them. Rather than focusing your letter on the physical things that person has (their looks or money), focus it on their personal qualities.**

_____|_____
_____|_____
_____|_____
_____|_____
_____|_____
_____|_____
_____|_____
_____|_____

Once you're done, replace their name with yours at the top. Assume for the time being that you wouldn't even have noticed those qualities in that person if they didn't already exist at some level in you. What is it about this person that is highlighting a quality or value you like? Could you bring out more of it in yourself? What would it look like in your everyday life to show one of those qualities yourself?

Complete this thought:

One small way I can use one of those qualities in my everyday life is. . .

Use Yourself as Your Reference Point

Every once and a while, like at the start of a new semester, your birthday, or a new year, make yourself your reference point. Answer these questions:

In what ways am I different now than how I was last (semester, year, birthday, etc.)?

What's different in my life now?

What do I do or know now that I didn't do or know then?

What improvements have I made that I can celebrate?

Manage Your Social Media Use

Use social media less. The research shows time on social media has neutral to negative effects on things that are important to our happiness and success. Those things include confidence, motivation, focus, and physical health.

If you use it, diversify your feed. Fill your follows with different kinds of reference points, so your perspective on reality isn't skewed toward the perfect.

Exercise 3: Practice Non-attachment

Here's a brief exercise to get less attached to the outcome of your dream and more attached to the positive effects of the dream itself. Admittedly, this one takes a lot of practice, but you'll get better at it the more you work on noticing it in yourself and others. Be kind and compassionate with your self-talk when you notice you've become attached to the outcome of something, and it's causing you stress or disappointment. You can say something like this to yourself: "Oh, look at me, being a normal human again! I notice I've been really attached to that outcome for my happiness. It's natural that I'm feeling frustrated or disappointed. And there are some small things I can do now to feel a little better."

Methods:

1. Have a dream.
2. Define feelings and beliefs.
3. Act that way right now.

Have a Dream

A dream I have for myself is. . .

Define Feelings and Beliefs

When you picture yourself in that dream, how do you feel?

What did you believe about yourself that made that dream possible?

Act That Way Right Now

If you already felt that way and believed those thoughts about yourself, how would you act differently right now?	

What's a single action you are willing to follow through doing? Schedule it, plan it, and make a reminder of it now.

I'm willing to. . .	

Myth 2: Happiness Is a Result of Achieving Success

Imagine you have dedicated your whole young life to becoming an elite athlete. You sacrifice and drive yourself to practice and improve around a busy school schedule. You dream of and visualize being an all-star champion. All of that sacrifice and hard work worked for Tal Ben-Shahar, at least in terms of becoming an elite athlete. But, later when he became a teacher of two of the most popular classes ever taught at Harvard about positive psychology, he reflected:

> "I thought if I win this tournament that then I'll be happy," he said. "And I won, and I was happy. And then the same stress and pressure and emptiness returned" (Shilton 2019).

He would later study this phenomenon that occurs with other high achieving individuals, celebrities, and athletes and termed it the *arrival fallacy*. It's what happens when you put all your happiness on hold to strive for an external marker of success, only to find that when you reach it, the happiness doesn't last, and you're still just the plain old you that you were before you reached the goal.

This isn't to scare you off from setting big, bright goals about what you want to do and have in your future. Those shiny objects can play a big role in positive motivation. The trick is to include one other important element our culture rarely emphasizes: how you want to be.

Coming Back to Values

Way back in the first section, you brainstormed words and actions to create habits that were in line with the type of person you wanted to be. Another word for that is your values. When I talk about values, I don't mean them in a moral, right-or-wrong sense. I think of values more as strengths — qualities you appreciate that make life meaningful. They strengthen you when you notice them in others and get to see them in your own actions and life. Over 20 years ago, a group of pioneering researchers and psychologists wanted to know if there were some common qualities that allowed humans across cultures to flourish. They spent three years traveling and researching this question. They developed 24 signature strengths or values that every human has to varying degrees. Those strengths and values promote individual happiness, well-being, and success, as well as the success of others in their community. In other words, these are qualities that make us feel and do better for ourselves and others — a win-win for you and society. You can find the list of those qualities and even take a free quiz online at the VIA Institute on Character. Their research continues to prove that when we connect these core, signature ways we wish to be as a person, these values that strengthen us, we end up improving things like academic performance, career success, feelings of satisfaction and happiness, relationships, and as a bonus for humanity, our communities, too.

Amy Wrzesniewski is a professor at Yale University who researches how individuals make their work feel more meaningful and personally fulfilling even in difficult circumstances. She proved the effectiveness of something she coined as *job crafting*, which means figuring out how to bring your values and signature strengths into your everyday tasks, no matter what they are. You don't have to be a star stand-up comedian to bring humor to your life every day and make others laugh. You don't need to be a Grammy-winning, platinum-selling musician to feel the joy and purpose in making music. You don't need to have thousands of Instagram followers on your fashion-focused IG account to appreciate the beauty of colors, patterns, and visual organization. Maybe those things are in store for you, but you don't have to wait until that happens to bring those values and strengths into your everyday tasks right now. In fact, the research shows that doing so will make you happier in your everyday life. It's also more likely that you'll have the motivation, awareness, and resilience to reach those goals in the long run.

The more ways you apply your values in everyday life, you end up reversing the myth that happiness is a byproduct of success. Success becomes a byproduct of being happier in your everyday life. Here are a few exercises to help.

Exercise 1: Set Voals Instead of Goals

Voles are cute, furry underground rodents. Sort of like a vole, a *voal* is something you tunnel down beneath the surface to find. It's a combination of your values plus your goals.

Method

1. Identify values.
2. Identify goals.
3. Put them together.
4. Notice and practice your values in small ways every day.

Identify Values

First, check out this bank of values that was developed by super famous research professor, author, and speaker Brené Brown for her Dare to Lead program that cultivates leadership qualities. I have whittled it down to the values that most of my students seem to gravitate toward for our purposes here, but I highly recommend checking out the full list on her website.

On the opposite page, highlight or circle the three you are drawn to most. Try not to think about this too hard. This could be because you already recognize yourself in that quality. But it could also be because it lifts your spirit to think about it, raises your curiosity, or makes you sit a little taller. These will change as you move through different phases in life, so this is a great exercise to do at the start of a new semester or year.

Know that you can't get this wrong, since you're always allowed to change your mind about it. So, once you've picked a quality, it shows you something you value.

	Write one to three words that describe values that matter to you below.
1	
2	
3	

MY VALUES

Accountability	Efficiency	Independence	Risk-taking
Achievement	Equality	Job security	Safety
Adventure	Fairness	Joy	Self-discipline
Ambition	Faith	Justice	Self-expression
Authenticity	Family	Kindness	Service
Balance	Financial stability	Leadership	Spirituality
Beauty	Freedom	Learning	Sportsmanship
Caring	Friendship	Love	Success
Collaboration	Fun	Loyalty	Teamwork
Commitment	Generosity	Making a difference	Travel
Community	Giving back	Nature	Truth
Compassion	Gratitude	Optimism	Uniqueness
Confidence	Growth	Peace	Wealth
Creativity	Health	Perseverance	Well-being
Curiosity	Honesty	Reliability	Wisdom
Diversity	Hope	Respect	Other:
Env ironment	Humor	Responsibility	Other:

Identify Your Goals

Okay, now you'll put your values together with your goals to make them extra meaningful and powerful. I don't get too picky about all the SMART goal rules, if you've been taught those. (I don't have anything against those rules, I just don't think they're necessary.) Just pick something for some time in the year ahead that you want to achieve that's a little bit of a stretch but seems possible.

My goal(s):	

Put Them Together

Now, join one of your values with a goal using the voal formula:

VOAL FORMULA

So that I can be _____ (value),

I will _____ (goal).

You can either plug that in from the work above or adjust the wording to be more specific. I recommend writing out a few until you have one to three that feel motivating and clear to you.

Examples:

- So that I can be creative, I will get homework in on time, so I will have free time on weekends to make music.
- So that I can be peaceful, I will keep up with organizing my time and stuff, so I know what's going on and can easily find things I need.
- So that I can be a good friend, I will get better sleep on a consistent basis, so I'm in a better mood.

Practice Values in Small Ways Every Day

Finally, what are some small ways you can put that value into action in your everyday life that would also help you toward your goal? For example, if your value was relaxed and your goal was getting your homework started by 5 pm to give yourself more free time, taking long naps is probably not going to be a great strategy for both of those things. But, doing a five-minute meditation when you get home from school might help with that. Or, taking a walk outside when you get home from school to clear your mind might help.

A few strategies that bring my value and my goal together are:	

Take one or two minutes a few times throughout the day to close your eyes and imagine the feeling of your value in your body. Doing this can start to train your nervous system to find and use that value automatically when you're going about your day.

Let's try that now:

When you feel _____ (name your value here), what does it feel like?	
Where in your body do you feel it?	
Once you have a sense of the feeling can you take just a moment or two to breathe it into yourself?	
Can you imagine it growing a little bigger as you breathe and spreading to your whole body?	

Exercise 2: Make a Daily To-Do and To-Be List

This one is best to do in the morning. So that you remember to do it and make it a habit, it's best to connect this with a morning routine you already have like eating breakfast, waiting for the bus, or sitting in your first period class waiting for class to start.

Method

1. Prioritize to-dos.
2. Connect it to your values.
3. Choose an anchor to remember it throughout the day.

Prioritize To-Dos

Use the table below (you can also use a sticky note, paper, or a bullet journal). On the left side, write down what you need to get done for the day. You can either go through your responsibilities in your mind or check your portals and notes and make a list from those.

TO DO	TO BE

Put stars next to the three most important. Ask yourself, if you could only get three things done today, which would you choose?

Connect It to Your Values

On the right side, write down one to three words to describe how you want to be today. Don't think too hard about this. Usually, the first words that pop into your head are the best ones to guide you through the day. They will relate to your innate values naturally.

Here's an example with my top three starred:

TO DO	TO BE
Make flashcards for math test	Reliable
Make an appointment in writing center	Consistent
★ Catch up on math homework	Relaxed
★ Bring water bottle to soccer practice	
Outline English rough draft	
Spanish homework	
★ Text carpool my schedule	

Choose an Anchor to Remember It Throughout the Day

Choose an *anchor* to help you remember any of those "being words" throughout the day. This is something you will be sure to see or hear or touch during the day that you can attach your being words to. I like to play a game where I use double numbers as a prompt for me to remember my being words. Another student of mine uses the color purple. Every time I see repeating numbers come up, like when I look at the time and it's 1:44 pm, for example, I'll take a moment to remember a value (today, my word is "open"), and try to feel it.

> **Bonus tip: As you're laying in bed before falling asleep, playback the movie of the day in your mind's eye, pausing on a moment or two when you were being the way you wanted to be.**

Exercise 3: Ideal schedule

In this exercise, you're going to make an ideal schedule for yourself. This is a great thing to do on a Sunday before the week starts. You can also do this at any point during the week. You might want to when you find yourself feeling like your life is getting to be one homework assignment and chore after another, or you feel like you have no idea what's going on and like your life is getting a bit out of your control.

Method

1. Gather up your portals of information.
2. Make a want to do and need to-do list.
3. Time box it.

Gather up Your Portals of Information

This is a great exercise to pair with something that makes you feel nice and comfy. Do this with some soothing music, a nice candle, a good snack, or a person you like and trust.

Now, open all the places where you get information about the stuff that needs your time and attention. Here's a list. Check all that apply for you. To make it even easier, add in any information you need about websites and passwords, so it's all in one place for the next time.

P.S. Sometimes a parent is the portal for some of these items.

INFORMATION PORTALS	INFORMATION I NEED
Sports schedules	
Doctor appointments	
Online posts about assignments	

INFORMATION PORTALS	INFORMATION I NEED
Clubs	
Teaching and tutor meeting schedules	
Vacations and school breaks	

Make a Want To-Do/Need To-Do List

Before doing any scheduling, take three to five minutes making your want to-do/need to-do lists. You don't have to do this from memory. I recommend starting with the want to-do side first.

Things that need my time and attention this week (assignments, appointments, chores, etc.)	Time estimate	Things I want to spend time doing to be a happy, healthy person (hobbies, self care, social time, sleep, etc.)	Time estimate

Time Box It

Now, you're going to create the time you need to be a happy, healthy person who gets their stuff done, too, by boxing out the time you need. In the schedule, start with the things you want to do. Plug them into their ideal times during the week. Use a pencil in case you need to adjust things to make it work once you layer in the next list.

Then, move to the things you need to do. Slot them into the available spaces in your calendar. Remember that you can also use time before school and during breaks, lunch, school, or study periods, if you want to free up more time later for your want to-do list.

Finally, shade or highlight all the want to do boxes one color and the need to do boxes a different color. Doing this usually helps you see how much of a balance you are striking in your schedule for the week ahead. When I do this with my students, we almost always find there is still plenty of white space left as a buffer for the unexpected.

EXAMPLE NEEDS AND WANTS

Need to do (for school)	Need to do (for physical/ mental health)	Want to do for fun
Go to classes	Morning (AM) treadmill	Video games
Homework	Afternoon (PM) treadmill	Hang out with friends
Studying	Writing	
	Sit down and think	

EXAMPLE IDEAL WEEKLY SCHEDULE

TIME	M	T	W	TH	F
6 AM	Wake up and get ready	Wake up and get ready	Wake up and get ready	Wake up and get ready	Wake up and get ready
7 AM	Leave for school @7:15	Leave for school @7:15	Leave for school @7:15	Leave for school @7:15	Leave for school @7:15
8 AM					
9 AM					
10 AM					
11 AM					
12 PM					
1 PM					

EXAMPLE IDEAL WEEKLY SCHEDULE

TIME	M	T	W	TH	F
2 PM					
3 PM					
4 PM	Rest/guided meditation app	Rest/guided meditation app	Rest/guided meditation app	Rest/guided meditation app	Hang out with friends
5 PM	Homework/study	Tricia tutoring			Psychology appointment
6 PM	Free time	Study group	Free time	Free time	
7 PM	Dinner	Dinner	Dinner	Dinner	Dinner
8 PM	PM treadmill and walking	PM treadmill and walking	PM treadmill and walking	PM treadmill and walking	PM treadmill and walking
9 PM	Finish homework	Finish homework	Finish homework	Finish homework	Shower/free time
10 PM	Video games	Video games	Video games	Video games	Video games
11 PM	Sleep	Sleep	Sleep	Sleep	Sleep

Now, try your own. There are also blank templates in the resources section.

MY NEEDS AND WANTS

Need to do (for school)	Need to do (for physical/ mental health)	Want to do for fun

MY IDEAL WEEKLY SCHEDULE

TIME	M	T	W	TH	F
6 AM					
7 AM					
8 AM					
9 AM					
10 AM					
11 AM					
12 PM					
1 PM					
2 PM					
3 PM					
4 PM					
5 PM					
6 PM					
7 PM					
8 PM					
9 PM					
10 PM					
11 PM					

Section 5 Reflection

Here's a quick review of the points we covered in this section:

MYTH: DREAM IT, DO IT	MYTH: HAPPINESS IS A RESULT OF SUCCESS
Take care of your body	Set voals instead of goals
Turn compare-despair into compare-care	Make a daily to-do/to-be list
Practice non-attachment	Make an ideal schedule

What are the main ideas or points that seem important to you?	Why is something you read about particularly important or relevant to you?
When might you use something you learned?	Who could you reach out to for help? Can you think of anyone you could help with something you learned?

P.S. Taking five minutes to fill out a what, who, when, why chart at the end of any section you've read for school is a quick way to make what you read stick. You can always substitute a different question to fit the reading, such as: What were the main points? Who were the most important people involved? When did the important things take place? Why does it matter?

In the conclusion, you'll find a template you can use to pull many of the ideas from this book and plan out your next steps. I recommend checking in with this, or something you make on your own, at least every six weeks. Schedule it in now as a recurring event, so you get a reminder or see it in your calendar or planner. Get a trusted friend or adult to check in with you about it if you can. And above all else, keep your steps small. Something that's a little bit of a stretch, but totally do-able.

GET COUNTERCULTURAL KEY TAKEAWAYS

Getting countercultural is about paying attention to what doesn't feel right about a situation and taking steps to not only make that better for yourself, but others, too.

1	We can challenge the "dream it, do it" myth by taking care of the wisdom of our bodies, not just our minds.
2	You are biologically programmed to compare yourself to others, but there are ways to compare that lift you up rather than make you feel less-than.
3	Non-attachment is a mindfulness method that helps you have a dream inspire you without letting the outcome of your efforts determine your happiness and well-being.
4	We can challenge the myth that only success brings happiness by finding happiness in the process of moving towards success, which luckily, helps us be more successful anyway.
5	Cultivating and applying values to your everyday actions helps your well-being and causes you to truly flourish in life.

WRAP UP & RESOURCES

Conclusion

Before we get to the one last exercise in the book to help you put all your aha moments together into a plan, I have one last potential obstacle to that might come up for you. I want you to be aware of it, so you can expect it and steer around it if it happens.

Be on the lookout for behaviors that take you back to your set point, the point where you are coasting, not changing much but not feeling all that great about things either. You see, your nervous system is designed to keep you safe. Hooray! To it, being safe means being comfy.

Okay, you may be thinking, I'm still not seeing a problem here. I like being comfortable. But, to your brain, being comfy means staying the same. If you're trying to change some deep patterns and habits, or if you're acting in ways that go against the status quo, your brain will throw up all its best tricks and obstacles to keep you exactly the same. It does this so you go along with what everyone else seems to be doing and saying and expecting from you. That's the way to stay alive. No sudden movements, stay under the radar, nothing to see here, and the predators won't find you.

Sometimes, there's a good reason to act that way, and it's okay. If something or someone is actively hurting you physically or emotionally, you might need to do that while you're getting help to protect yourself. You might also need a temporary time to rest and restore after a period of big challenges and change.

But if that's not your situation and you start sliding back into old ways keeping you from trying something that could make you feel happier and work better, then you're going to want to deal with that. Here are a few of my favorite ways to handle the slide back to your set point:

1. **Be aware of it and expect it to happen.**
   I think this feeling of wanting to slide back to my old ways of taking a nap right after school is my brain being afraid of the changes I'm making to become more successful.

2. **Negotiate when it comes up.**
   The key here is not trying to push past without acknowledging that pesky voice that tempts you to go back to old ways. Give it some space to be heard and seen. Journal about it. Talk with someone. Keeping your goals in mind, treat it like an annoying but cute puppy you have to reassure from time to time. *Alright, brain, I see you trying to make me slide back. We're not doing that this time. This is good for us. You'll see.*

3. **Join or create your own support group.**
   A tiny step towards doing this is to tell someone you trust about what you're trying and ask them to help by checking in with you every week to see how it's going. *Maybe I'll ask my advisor at school to ask me every Friday if I was able to avoid napping before starting homework that week.*

The ideas and strategies in this book are ones I still come back to in my own life, and I am waaaay out of school. I want you to know that ups and downs are to be expected, as long as you're a human being reading this and not an alien from the future. The alien who found this is probably laughing at how easy it was to take over our planet because we humans were so flawed with our ever-present propensity to make mistakes, get distracted, and have feelings. So, until the aliens take over, and we're still running things around here, you get to have the fun of looking at each day as a new try (or even each new hour if you're having that kind of day).

Now to pull your learning together and make it something you can put into action in your life. Here's a final exercise. Feel free to do this on your own or grab a positive partner with good ideas who you trust to help you.

Final Exercise: Value and Habit Idea Explosion

You will need two things:

- The mind map below (or a blank piece of paper)
- A fresh habit tracker (like the one on the next page)

Method

1. Mind map your values.
2. Brainstorm actions and strategies.
3. Identify the two Es.
4. Put some actions and strategies into a habit tracker.
5. Set up a remember-to-remember system.

Mind Map Your Values

Draw a circle in the center of a blank page. Write in one to three values about how you want to be in life to be truly happy and successful. There have been lots of activities we've done before to help you come up with these things, so hopefully it will be easy for you to pick a few.

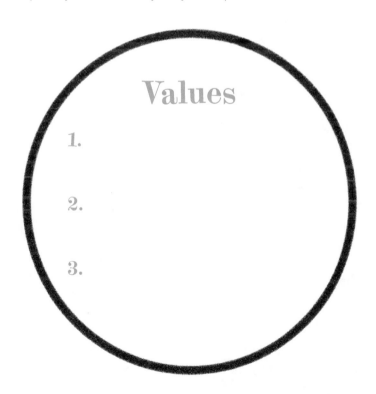

Values

1.

2.

3.

Brainstorm Actions and Strategies

Set a timer for three minutes. Grab some sticky notes or write these around your values on the page. Brainstorm all the actions, habits, behaviors, strategies, and tricks that would help you be more like those values. Go back through your notes from this course and incorporate any of the tips and strategies that seem like a good idea and feel free to get creative and come up with your own.

Take a few deep breaths. You're doing great!

Identify the Two Es: Easy and Effective

Now, put a star next to the three that you think would be the most effective in getting you towards your goals. Then, put a star next to the three that you think would be the easiest to implement.

Put Some Actions and Strategies into a Habit Tracker

If you're lucky, you'll have one or two that have double stars! You'll want to put those in your habit tracker now. Those are definite winners. If not, apply this question: Is there a way you can make one of the most effective habits easier by making it into a smaller step? If so, do that now and add it to your habit tracker as well. Here's another habit tracker to get you started:

HABIT	1	2	3	4	5	6	7

Set Up a Remember-to-Remember System

Here are some suggestions. I'll keep track of how I'm following through on these by (check all that apply or come up with your own remember-to-remember system):

✓	REMEMBER-TO-REMEMBER SYSTEMS
	Keeping my habit tracker visible and checking it off each day
	Having someone I trust to check in with me about it each week
	Wearing a string around my wrist to remind me of my habits

✓	REMEMBER-TO-REMEMBER SYSTEMS
	Setting reminders on my phone and/or computer
	Writing encouraging Post-it notes about the habits and putting them in places I'll see often
	Holding a mini celebration for myself each time I follow through
	Setting up a reward if I follow through the majority of the time each week
	Attaching the new habit to something I already always do, like when I eat breakfast (something I always do), I'll write my top three priorities for the day on a notecard to keep in my pocket (new habit)
	Other:

All Set Now, Right?

I'd like to tell you that you're all set now. It'll be smooth sailing from here on out. Stick to these strategies and you'll never have another day of uncertainty, boredom, frustration, or distress. You're probably old enough by now not to buy that statement.

So, instead, I want to leave you with this practice I have in my own life that has served me well. There are going to be days when things just go off the rails. Practice runs into the time you designated for your homework. A parent needs you to drive your sibling to music lessons, which breaks up your study flow or happens right when you had planned to take a break for yourself. The teacher gives a test with totally unexpected questions you hadn't prepared for. A pandemic shuts down school. Life will have its way of throwing off our very well-intentioned and well-thought-through routines, habits, and even mindsets. Most of the time, our systems and healthy mindsets will work. Sometimes though, stuff happens, and we have to let go of our plans and tried-and-true strategies.

When that happens, come back to your values. Rely on the things you truly care about that motivate you to get up and make life meaningful to you. I have zero experience with the military, but I do like the idea of marching orders when it comes to values. Officially, these are a set of instructions someone in command gives to their group before sending them out on a mission. The message is no matter what, stick to these simple, easy-to-remember instructions to stay on track. For our purposes in this book, those commands are the deep, wise self every one of us has inside, and the mission is finding joy and success on your own unique terms.

If you can, try to put your values into a simple set of one to four marching orders on how to live your life day-to-day. So, even when things throw your plans up into the air, you know what you can fall back on to stay on track. Let's say you really value being relaxed. Your marching order for that could be, "Breathe and center yourself in calm as often as you can." Or maybe one of your values is being responsible. Your marching order for that might be, "Evaluate your choices and make a plan." It will look different depending on what you care about and what makes you feel clear and inspired. I come back to my marching orders multiple times a day.

It's possible that you need a little more time and experience to find marching orders that work for you. So, if you try this and come up a little fuzzy and confused, please don't stress about it. I'm happy to give you mine as a loaner until one day yours become clear. I struggled (and still do) with almost all of the issues addressed in this book in my own life. These have worked to pull me through many difficult moments big and small.

My Marching Orders:

- Show up with loving, present-moment awareness.
- Have fun learning and creating new things.
- Help others.
- Soak in all the good.

Rights and Wrongs

I have one last cultural norm I want you to be aware of and question if you see it coming up in your mind. We tend to think in terms of rights and wrongs. *Getting my homework done while sitting at a desk between the hours of 4 and 6 pm is the right way to do it. If I don't do it that way, I'm doing it wrong.* Even the title of this book might be misleading. Some of you might be thinking that if you just follow the exact steps in this book, it will be the secret to your success. In truth, there are no exact right or wrong steps to follow. The pillars in this book are mindsets and strategies you can use to decorate whatever path you happen to follow to make it more interesting, fun, or easier to walk.

Getting hung up on trying to guess the right path to take can leave you frozen with fear of stepping out of line. There are so many paths when you find more peace, connection, and play. They can all be the "right" ones because they keep you moving. It's the forward action that creates the stuff we need for success like momentum, confidence, and resilience. Even if you take a few steps in that direction and find it was a mistake, you've learned not to go that way again. Great!

The truth is any path you choose is the right one, because you get to make it great with each step. Even when you make mistakes, you get to choose how you want to move forward.

Which steps will you take today? I can't wait for you to find out!

> **I'd love to continue to support you along this path to more happiness and success. Please visit triciaunderwood.com to learn how to connect with me and find more resources and services.**

Resources

Downloads

Visit h2c.ai/hgw for downloads.

Bibliography

Achacoso, Michelle V. 2004. "Post-Test Analysis: A Tool for Developing Students' Metacognitive Awareness and Self-Regulation." New Directions for Teaching and Learning 2004 (100): 115–19. https://doi.org/10.1002/tl.179.

Alva, Sylvia Alatorre. 1991. "Academic Invulnerability Among Mexican-American Students: The Importance of Protective Resources and Appraisals." Hispanic Journal of Behavioral Sciences 13 (1): 18–34. https://doi.org/10.1177/07399863910131002.

Beck, Martha. 2021. *The Way of Integrity: Finding the Path to Your True Self*. The Open Field.

Brach, Tara. "Working With Difficulties: The Blessings of RAIN." Tara Brach. Last modified July 1, 2011. https://www.tarabrach.com/rain-workingwithdifficulties/.

Brown, Brené. "Dare to Lead List of Values." Brené Brown. Last modified August 13, 2023. https://brenebrown.com/resources/dare-to-lead-list-of-values/.

Cain, Susan. 2012. *Quiet: The Power of Introverts in a World That Can't Stop Talking*. Crown Publishing Group.

Clear, James M. 2018. *Atomic Habits: An Easy & Proven Way to Build Good Habits & Break Bad Ones*. Avery.

Dweck, Carol S. 2007. *Mindset: The New Psychology of Success*. Ballantine Books.

Eurich, Tasha. 2023. "What Self-Awareness Really Is (and How to Cultivate It)." *Harvard Business Review*, January 4, 2018. Accessed April 6, 2023. https://hbr.org/2018/01/what-self-awareness-really-is-and-how-to-cultivate-it.

Fredrickson, Barbara L. 2001. "The Role of Positive Emotions in Positive Psychology: The Broaden-and-Build Theory of Positive Emotions." American Psychologist 56 (3): 218–26. https://doi.org/10.1037/0003-066x.56.3.218.

Garcia, Patricia. 2018. "Serena Williams Shares Her Struggle With Postpartum Depression on Instagram." *Vogue*, August 7, 2018. https://www.vogue.com/article/serena-williams-motherhood-postpartum-disorders-instagram.

Hanh, Thich Nhat. 2023. *How to Smile*. Parallax Press.

Hanson, Rick, PhD. 2013. *Hardwiring Happiness: The New Brain Science of Contentment, Calm, and Confidence*. Harmony.

"Jack Needs Jill to Get Up the Hill: Perceptions Affected by Friendship." *The University of Virginia Magazine*, Fall 2009. https://uvamagazine.org/articles/jack_needs_jill_to_get_up_the_hill.

Jha, Amishi. 2021. *Peak Mind: Find Your Focus, Own Your Attention, Invest 12 Minutes a Day*. Hachette Audio UK.

Kelley, David, and Tom Kelley. 2013. *Creative Confidence: Unleashing the Creative Potential Within Us All*. Crown.

Levitin, Daniel J. 2015. "Why It's So Hard To Pay Attention, Explained By Science." Fast Company, September. https://www.fastcompany.com/3051417/why-its-so-hard-to-pay-attention-explained-by-science.

MindShift. "The Role of Metacognition in Learning and Achievement." KQED. Last modified August 10, 2016. https://www.kqed.org/mindshift/46038/the-role-of-metacognition-in-learning-and-achievement.

Molfino, Majo. 2020. *Break the Good Girl Myth: How to Dismantle Outdated Rules, Unleash Your Power, and Design a More Purposeful Life*. HarperOne.

"More than Just Memories: A New Role for the Hippocampus during Learning." 2019. ScienceDaily. March 19, 2019. https://www.sciencedaily.com/releases/2019/03/190306081704.htm.

Neff, Kristin. 2011. *Self-Compassion: The Proven Power of Being Kind to Yourself*. Harper Collins.

Oettingen, Gabriele. 2014. *Rethinking Positive Thinking: Inside the New Science of Motivation*. Penguin.

Paul, Annie Murphy. 2021. *The Extended Mind: The Power of Thinking Outside the Brain*. HarperCollins.

Potash, Betsy. "A Simple Trick for Success with One-Pagers." Cult of Pedagogy. Last modified May 26, 2019. https://www.cultofpedagogy.com/one-pagers/.

Price, Catherine. 2018. *How to Break Up With Your Phone: The 30-Day Plan to Take Back Your Life*. Ten Speed Press.

Robinson, Ken, Sir. "Do schools kill creativity?" Speech presented at TED, 2006. Video. TED. Posted February 2006. https://www.ted.com/talks/sir_ken_robinson_do_schools_kill_creativity/ transcript.

Schuster, Tara. 2020. *Buy Yourself the F*cking Lilies: And Other Rituals to Fix Your Life, from Someone Who's Been There*. Dial Press.

Sharf, Zack. 2023. "Marie Kondo Has 'Kind of Given up' on Tidying Up: 'My Home Is Messy.'" *Variety*, January 27, 2023. https://variety.com/2023/tv/news/marie-kondo-stops-tidying-up-home-messy-1235504610/.

Shilton, A. C. "You Accomplished Something Great. So Now What?" *The New York Times*, May 28, 2019. https://www.nytimes.com/2019/05/28/smarter-living/you-accomplished-something-great-so-now-what.html.

Sincero, Jen. 2020. *Badass Habits: Cultivate the Awareness, Boundaries, and Daily Upgrades You Need to Make Them Stick*. Penguin Life.

Taylor, Jill Bolte. 2021. *Whole Brain Living: The Anatomy of Choice and the Four Characters That Drive Our Life*. Hay House, Inc.

"The Science of Well-Being for Teens." Coursera. 2023. https://www.coursera.org/learn/the-science-of-well-being-for-teens.

"VIA Character Strengths Survey & Character Reports." VIA Institute on Character. 2023. https://viacharacter.org.

Vo, Dzung X. 2015. *The Mindful Teen: Powerful Skills to Help You Handle Stress One Moment at a Time*. New Harbinger Publications.

Westhoff, Bianca, Iris J. Koele, and Ilse van de Groep. 2020. "Social Learning and the Brain: How Do We Learn From and About Other People?" Frontiers for Young Minds, August. https://doi.org/10.3389/frym.2020.00095.

Wrzesniewski, Amy, and Jane E. Dutton. 2001. "Crafting a Job: Revisioning Employees as Active Crafters of Their Work." The Academy of Management Review 26 (2): 179–201. https://doi.org/10.5465/amr.2001.4378011.

Recommended Reading

Achor, Shawn. 2018. *Big Potential: How Transforming the Pursuit of Success Raises Our Achievement, Happiness, and Well-Being*. Currency.

Biegel, Gina M. 2020. *Take in the Good: Skills for Staying Positive and Living Your Best Life*. Shambhala Publications.

Dawson, Peg. 2010. *Executive Skills in Children and Adolescents: A Practical Guide to Assessment and Intervention*. The Guilford Press.

Diamond, Adele, and Kathleen Lee. 2011. "Interventions Shown to Aid Executive Function Development in Children 4 to 12 Years Old." Science 333 (6045): 959–64. https://doi.org/10.1126/science.1204529.

Dunstan, Julie, and Susannah Cole. 2021. *Flexible Mindsets in Schools: Channelling Brain Power for Critical Thinking, Complex Problem-Solving and Creativity*. Routledge.

Feldman, Joe. 2018. *Grading for Equity: What It Is, Why It Matters, and How It Can Transform Schools and Classrooms*. Corwin Press.

Hammond, Zaretta. 2014. *Culturally Responsive Teaching and The Brain: Promoting Authentic Engagement and Rigor Among Culturally and Linguistically Diverse Students*. Corwin Press.

Kleon, Austin. 2012. *Steal Like an Artist: 10 Things Nobody Told You About Being Creative*. Workman Publishing Company.

Kotler, Steven. 2021. *The Art of Impossible: A Peak Performance Primer*. Harper Wave.

Love, Bettina L. 2019. *We Want to Do More Than Survive: Abolitionist Teaching and the Pursuit of Educational Freedom*. Beacon Press.

Muhammad, Gholdy. 2023. *Unearthing Joy: A Guide to Culturally and Historically Responsive Teaching and Learning*. Scholastic Teaching Solutions.

Ritchhart, Ron, Mark Church, and Karin Morrison. 2011. *Making Thinking Visible: How to Promote Engagement, Understanding, and Independence for All Learners*. Jossey-Bass.

Tomlinson, Carol Ann, and Jay McTighe. 2006. *Integrating Differentiated Instruction & Understanding by Design: Connecting Content and Kids*. ASCD.

Glossary

amygdala — a specific region of the brain that is the earliest to develop and is responsible for immediate, emotional reactions. It plays a big role in controlling emotion, motivation, and memory. The teenage and young adult brain is more guided by this emotional and reactive region than the logical, thoughtful prefrontal cortex.

anchor —an item you designate that reminds you of something when you see or touch it throughout the day, a physical memory device.

ANTs (automatic negative thoughts) — repetitive thoughts that we tend to use against ourselves for a good reason.

arrival fallacy — when you put all your happiness on hold to strive for an external marker of success, only to find that when you reach it, the happiness doesn't last, and you're still just the plain old you that you were before you reached the goal.

cognition — your ability to think clearly.

compare-despair cycle — when comparing ourselves to others leads to putting ourselves down, feeling insecure, and feeling unmotivated in attempts to improve our lives.

co-regulation — the psychological phenomenon that explains how our emotions and behaviors are contagious to others near us.

dopamine, oxytocin, serotonin, and endorphins — a family of feel-good chemicals in the nervous system that help us to feel peaceful, happy, motivated, confident, and positive connections to others.

empathy — being in tune with the emotions of others, an ability to accurately imagine and understand what others are thinking or feeling.

habit — an action, thought, or feeling that you repeat so many times that it becomes something you do, think, or feel without even trying.

hippocampus — a small but mighty part of our brain responsible for storing long-term memories. It is deeply connected with our sensory system, so the more physical senses are involved in an experience, the stronger it will store the memory long-term.

interdependence — connecting with others in ways that benefit all involved.

job crafting — figuring out how to bring your values and strengths into your everyday tasks.

marching orders — a set of instructions someone in command gives to their group before sending them on a mission; the deep, wise self every one of us has inside with the mission of finding joy and success on your own unique terms.

metacognition — when you think about how you think and learn.

microburst — short, deliberate, and focused period of working on something.

mindfulness — paying attention to what you are sensing in the present moment without judgment or criticism.

motivation — the reason for acting in a certain way. You can create motivation through action.

negativity bias — our tendency to hold onto memories about the negative more than the positive as a security mechanism to keep us safe and away from threat and danger.

non-attachment — a positive coping mechanism where you let go of your expectation about the outcome of your action.

novelty — something that feels new and fresh.

personal guidance system — the physical body as a source of wisdom for knowing what feels right or wrong.

problem pressing — a tendency to make unpleasant circumstances worse by making them mean something worse about who we are or what might happen as a result.

proclamation — a public statement about something important.

prototype — A smaller, test version of something. Usually a creative design for a product, but in our case, a prototype can also be a habit or strategy.

reference point — an object, for our purposes this means a person, who we use as a point of comparison to determine how we are doing. Psychologically, we have a really annoying tendency to pick reference points that make us feel like we'll never be, do, or have enough.

resilience — the ability to recover from setbacks and adversity with positive coping in a way where you continue to move toward meaningful goals.

reticular activating system (RAS) — a cluster of cells in our brains that processes new incoming information. It controls our awareness, so we can act in certain ways to keep our beliefs and identities safe.

self-compassion — an attitude that involves treating yourself with kindness and understanding in difficult times. It includes recognizing that making mistakes is just part of being human.

self-efficacy — having confidence in your own abilities and believing you have the power to accomplish things in different areas of your life

sketchnotes — a visual way of taking notes that combines text with simple drawings and doodles

unscheduling — purposely blocking out time in your schedule to do something fun and relaxing. Lets your brain know it has time for the things it wants to do, so it goes easier on you when you have to do something.

values — qualities you appreciate that make life meaningful. They strengthen you when you notice, experience, or use them in your actions. Standards that you believe are important in life.

voals — a combination of your values and your goals.

Acknowledgements

If you've read this far, you probably know that I'm a big believer in appreciation and gratitude. That's why it might come as a surprise that I am writing my acknowledgements at the absolute last minute. Every other part of this book I have drafted, reworked and edited, right on time, sometimes even early, but this has been by far the hardest for me to face due to my deep fear of leaving someone out. How to even start acknowledging all of the caring, wise, and influential people in my life who have helped me create this book? But, it's way too important to skip, so, I'm taking my own advice from this book and chunking it into tiny parts, intentionally keeping this small because if I endeavor to acknowledge everyone, I think my brain will explode and the terror of leaving someone out will get the better of me.

I'll start with my first teachers, my parents, Everett and Irene Porter. They taught me hard work as a value. They also taught me to value laughter and play even in the face of great adversity. These are values that have left their mark all over the themes of this book.

To my children, Finch and Molly, the most adorable, loving teachers one could ask for. You force me to learn the difference between choosing actions based on love over fear again and again in this wild experience of trying to be the parent you need.

To my husband, Matt. Beyond keeping my life together and serving as my left brain, you also bring such joy and optimism to my day when I get mired in worry over all my inadequacies. I would most definitely not be in this wonderful place without you.

To my work spouses Morgan Potts and Rachel Peterson. Morgan, you have been a consistent source of all the best things to learn about in this field. If Morgan suggests it, I know it's going to be high quality. I'm so happy we've made the professional to personal leap with our friendship. Rachel, you believed in this book when it was a glorified draft. Your encouragement has elevated my work and pushed me to make it better. I can only pray that I return the favor in some small way in our friendship.

To Becky McCleery whose expertise in online business and project management helped me break down this project and others into manageable steps. Her gentle and wise spirit guided me forward and gave me a soft place to land when stepping into the wilderness of creating something new to share with others felt overwhelming. If you have an online business project you want to bring to life, please look her up: www.linkedin.com/in/becky-lyter-mccleery/.

To Martha Beck for creating the class on creativity that gave life to this idea, and who taught me how to detect that pull forward that I should follow even when it doesn't seem practical. Learning how to tune in to that "pull" is the most practical sort of magic that works every time in my life.

And speaking of practical magic, thank you to Sonia Fox Fuller who casually mentioned that she knew of a local publisher who might be interested in this project when we were swapping some advice over coffee. Thank you for generously giving your time and advice that day.

To the very talented, sweet, and supportive team at How2Conquer publishing. All first time authors should be so lucky to be guided through this process with warmth and patience like I have experienced with Michelle Newcome, Lauren Kelliher, Charlotte Bleau, Emily Owens, and Telia Garner. Your sharp insights and creative design has made this something I am excited to share, and your care for your authors comes through in all your communication and guidance. Michelle Newcome, thank you for taking a chance on a first-time author and creating an indie, nonfiction publisher so that authors like me could have this opportunity. I am ridiculously grateful for all the serendipitous moments that led to me finding you and taking this from a pet project to a professional book. Thank you for creating something I want to share and giving it potential to help others who find it.

Which brings me to you, the readers! Thank you for picking this up and having the optimism and curiosity to see what you can make better in your life and the lives of others you care for.

About the Author

Tricia Underwood, M.A.T., is a joy-centered executive functioning specialist, entrepreneur, in the most creative sense of the word, and writer. She has been an inclusion teacher and professional development facilitator in public, private, and charter schools for 20 years. Tricia now brings her unique teaching/coaching blend to students, parents, and educators outside of those traditional classroom walls.

She loves to learn, read, and write about the art and science of the pursuit of joy. Her interest lies in how to use that to help students become mindfully productive in reaching meaningful goals for themselves. When she's not helping clients and brainstorming her next book projects, she has as much fun as she can manage with friends and family in Atlanta, reading all the fiction and personal development books, and taking her clumsy dog on walks. You can find out more at triciaunderwood.com.

Templates

Visit h2c.ai/hgw to download more!

HABIT	1	2	3	4	5	6	7

HABIT	1	2	3	4	5	6	7

HABIT	1	2	3	4	5	6	7

Simple Time Manager

M	T
Homework:	Homework:
W	Th
Homework:	Homework:
F	Sa/Su
Homework:	Homework:

Next Week

Simple Time Manager

M	T
Homework:	Homework:
W	Th
Homework:	Homework:
F	Sa/Su
Homework:	Homework:

Next Week

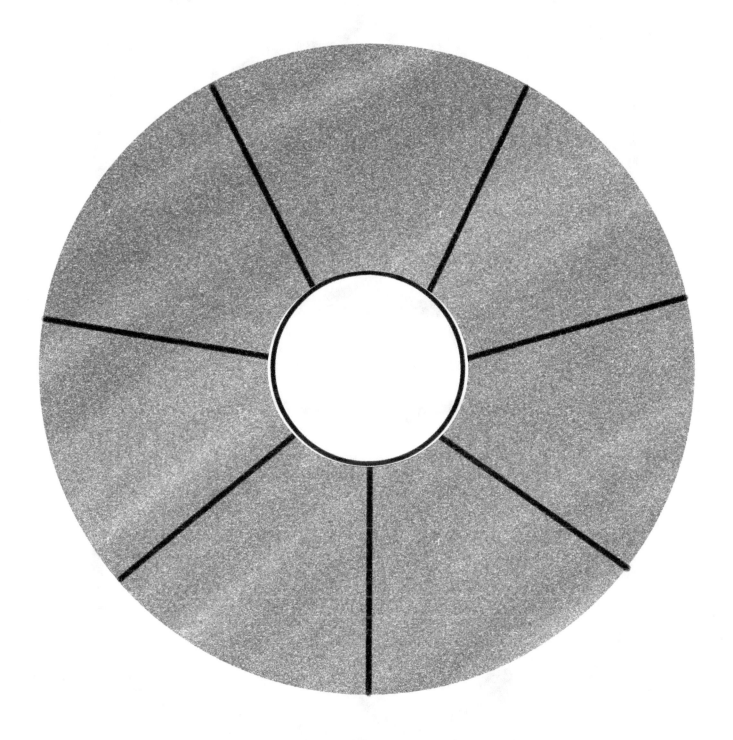

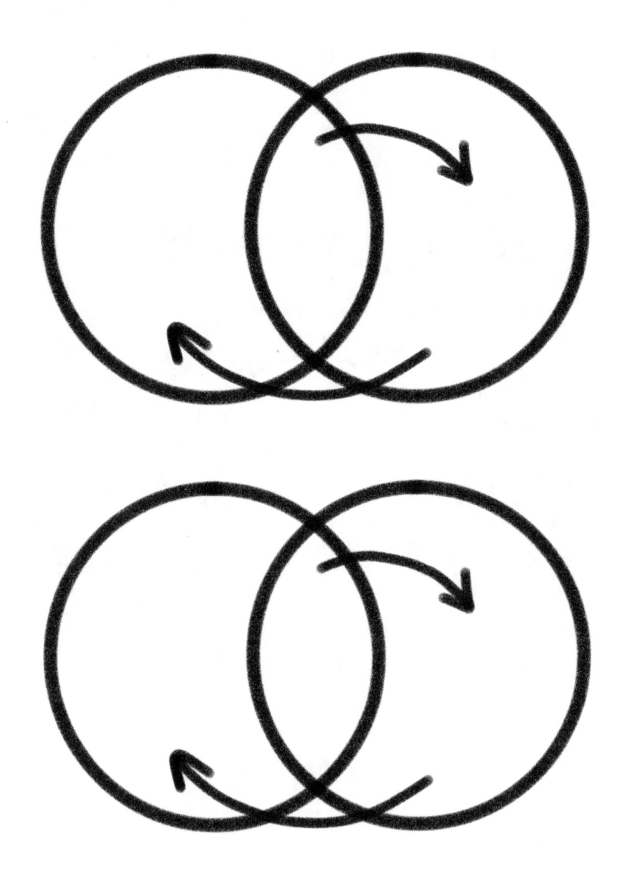

THE CHARACTER(S)	PERSONALITY TRAIT	WHAT DO THEY WANT?	WHAT GETS IN THEIR WAY?	HAPPY OR SAD ENDING FOR THEM?

NON-JUDGMENTAL POST-TEST CHECK-IN

Grade/score I wanted to get:	
Grade/score I got:	
What parts did I do well on?	
What parts did I miss?	
How many days in advance did I start studying?	
What methods did I use to study?	

NON-JUDGMENTAL POST-TEST CHECK-IN

Grade/score I wanted to get:	
Grade/score I got:	
What parts did I do well on?	
What parts did I miss?	
How many days in advance did I start studying?	
What methods did I use to study?	

NON-JUDGMENTAL POST-TEST CHECK-IN

Grade/score I wanted to get:	
Grade/score I got:	
What parts did I do well on?	
What parts did I miss?	
How many days in advance did I start studying?	
What methods did I use to study?	

PLANNING FOR THE NEXT TEST

Next test topic			Date	

What do I know about the format of the test?

What materials do I have that would be useful to study?

What methods do I want to use?
See the strategy chart on the next page for help!

What methods do I want to use to study?

4 days before test	
3 days before test	
2 days before test	
1 day before test	

PLANNING FOR THE NEXT TEST

On test day

How will I remember to take these steps on those days? (Go ahead and set your reminders, write in your planner, or tattoo it on your hand now.)

What other steps can I take to increase my motivation to follow through on this plan?

PLANNING FOR THE NEXT TEST

Next test topic		Date	

What do I know about the format of the test?

What materials do I have that would be useful to study?

What methods do I want to use?
See the strategy chart on the next page for help!

What methods do I want to use to study?

4 days before test	
3 days before test	
2 days before test	
1 day before test	

PLANNING FOR THE NEXT TEST

On test day

How will I remember to take these steps on those days? (Go ahead and set your reminders, write in your planner, or tattoo it on your hand now.)

What other steps can I take to increase my motivation to follow through on this plan?

TO DO	TO BE

TO DO	TO BE

TO DO	TO BE

INFORMATION PORTALS	INFORMATION I NEED

INFORMATION PORTALS	INFORMATION I NEED

INFORMATION PORTALS	INFORMATION I NEED

Things that need my time and attention this week (assignments, appointments, chores, etc.)	Time estimate

Things I want to spend time doing to be a happy, healthy person (hobbies, self care, social time, sleep, etc.)	Time estimate

MY NEEDS AND WANTS

Need to do (for school)	Need to do (for physical/ mental health)	Want to do for fun

MY IDEAL WEEKLY SCHEDULE

TIME	M	T	W	TH	F
6 AM					
7 AM					
8 AM					
9 AM					
10 AM					
11 AM					
12 PM					
1 PM					
2 PM					
3 PM					
4 PM					
5 PM					
6 PM					
7 PM					
8 PM					
9 PM					
10 PM					
11 PM					

Printed in the USA
CPSIA information can be obtained
at www.ICGtesting.com
LVHW080225151023
761014LV00071B/1273